Australia's Early Dwellings and Churches

AUSTRALIA'S EARLY DWELLINGS AND CHURCHES

PAINTINGS BY
Richard A. Smolicz

TEXT BY
W. Watson Sharp

Angus & Robertson Publishers

ANGUS & ROBERTSON PUBLISHERS
London . Sydney . Melbourne

First published in Australia by
Angus & Robertson Publishers in 1983
Reprinted 1984

Copyright © R. A. Smolicz and
W. Watson Sharp, 1983

National Library of Australia
Cataloguing-in-publication data.

Watson Sharp, W. (William), 1905—
    Australia's early dwellings and churches.

    ISBN 0 207 14726 4.

    1. Architecture, Domestic — Australia — History.
    2. Dwellings — Australia — History.
    3. Church architecture — Australia — History.
    4. Churches — Australia — History.
    I. Smolicz, R.A. (Richard Arkadiusz), 1923—
    II. Title.

728'.0994

Typeset in 11 pt Garamond
Printed in Hong Kong

We dedicate this book to our wives, Danuta and Mae, whom we dragged all over Australia. They acted as navigators, interrogators, note takers, packers, sympathisers, pacifiers, secretaries, accountants, relief drivers, and general factotums. They have demanded, and have received, nothing in return.

Foreword

Many of the grandiose homes built in Australia from the early years of European settlement have been preserved and extensively documented.

Imposing homes were built, particularly in the middle decades of the nineteenth century, by the new landed gentry quickly taking up large grants of land and numerous convict labourers.

Many complaints had reached London about the administration of Governor Macquarie (1810-1821) and so in 1819 John Thomas Bigge (formerly Governor of Trinidad) was appointed with a wide brief to recommend what sort of society and civilisation should develop in Australia. His recommendations substantially altered the land grant system. Bigge advocated, amongst other things, that 'settlers possessing capital' should receive grants of land with the area determined by the number of convicts they were prepared to employ. He also recommended the abolition of land grants to emancipists (ex-convicts). These suggestions were readily accepted as they relieved the British authorities of the responsibility of clothing, feeding and housing a large number of convicts.

Consequently, a small minority of families developed into a landed aristocracy with the wealth and labour to build large and gracious houses, many in a version of the English Georgian style. These have survived the test of time to be recorded in our architectural histories.

But the real pioneer homes of Australia were those built by under-privileged settlers — many of them escaped convicts — who ventured out into the wilderness and carved holdings for themselves out of the virgin and inhospitable bush.

Their homes were built without the benefit of skilled designers or tradesmen and with the absolute minimum of tools and equipment. Most of them, by the very nature of their construction and crude materials, have long since disappeared, their historical value unappreciated and their usefulness dissipated.

But here and there one comes across these reminders of a robust past, sometimes with one or two newer homesteads in the immediate proximity, or even more rarely still in use.

This book is an attempt to preserve in pictures and words typical examples of these fast-disappearing relics of our colourful past — humble dwellings and the equally simple places of worship fashioned by the pioneers.

The dwellings and churches pictured were standing at the time the paintings were made unless otherwise mentioned in the text. The sequence of presentation has been determined by the dates of the main settlements in each State. Dates given are in some cases approximate and are as accurate as it was possible to obtain.

Born in Poland and trained in art in England, Richard Smolicz took particular delight in the contrast of the new world with the old when he arrived in Australia in 1957.

Not only were there differences in light, colour and form but, coming from countries with their thousands of years of civilisation, Richard soon found himself intrigued by the opportunity to study and absorb a history and a culture which he was able to see from its beginning — at least from white man's beginning. He quickly developed a rapport with the Australian atmosphere as portrayed in its buildings and felt an urge to capture and record it on paper. It was, however, only after several years of occasional painting that the idea of publishing his recordings in book form came to him.

When Richard invited me to collaborate in the venture and to prepare the text to accompany his paintings he felt that my background as architect, author and editor might be helpful. Neither he nor I had any idea of what was involved.

He had already made perhaps one-fifth of the paintings. There had been no need to record the exact locations of these at the time, so when I set out to find them I discovered many of his directions sketchy to say the least — or perhaps I was a poor pathfinder. He had come on most of them by chance and could not always remember just where.

Our association led to 18 months of concentrated effort, searching out suitable subjects, Richard painting them and I researching their history and background. Many are neglected, the value of most unappreciated. Some, of course, are in the care of Historical Societies or the National Trust

and here the task was relatively easy. But in many cases local inquiries met with little or no success, people living alongside these valuable relics being unaware of their significance, often of their existence.

But there were also many who gave invaluable help in the preparation of this book and we acknowledge with gratitude the following: Miss Cecily Bell, Mostowie, Qld; Patrick Briody, Ercildoun, Vic; Canberra and District Historical Society, ACT; Fr N. A. Connell, Clunes, Vic; Fr Alan Corry MSC, Darwin, NT; Keith Cunningham, Wilberforce, NSW; Ron Cull, Albany, WA; Rev J. Drummett, Ilford, NSW; Mr and Mrs R. B. Dunbabin, Mayfield, Tas; Mrs Mary French, Stanley, Tas; Mrs Jean E. Glover, Auburn, SA; Cyril Gurney, Nullarbor, WA; Mrs Ada Elizabeth Lea, Norseman, WA; Brian Lambert, Katherine, NT; R. L. Robertson, Talbot, Vic; J. A. Maddock, Blue Mountains, NSW; Mr and Mrs Austin O'Malley, Ercildoun, Vic; Ben Paech, Kadina, SA; Mrs L. Parson, Jerramungup, WA; Mrs I. J. Sharp, Darling Downs, Qld; Tamworth Historical Society, NSW; Gordon Thomas, Ravensthorpe, WA; Sergeant of Police, Ravensthorpe, WA; Police Officer, Somerset, Tas.

W. Watson Sharp
Springwood
1983

Contents

Introduction

On 20 January 1788, a flotilla of 11 ships sailed into Botany Bay to establish the British colony of New South Wales. Under the command of Captain Arthur Phillip, there were 1487 people on board, almost 800 of them convicts.

Six days later, after having decided Botany Bay was unsuitable for settlement, Phillip led his flotilla north. He turned through commanding headlands into Port Jackson, which he described as 'a magnificent harbour, probably the most beautiful in the world'.

Eighteen years earlier Lieutenant James Cook had reached the east coast of Australia and landed at Botany Bay. He explored the area and then sailed on. He noted the Heads, named the estuary he knew must be there, Port Jackson, but did not enter.

Captain Phillip selected as a landing place a pleasant but thickly wooded cove which he named Sydney after the Home Secretary. He was influenced by a stream of fresh water flowing into it, following the age-old rule of water first, then shelter.

Phillip is reported as 'being hampered by lack of artificers' in the task of providing shelter for almost 1500 people. He set the ships' carpenters to work to build huts for the marines, while 70 to 100 convicts were assigned to build their own quarters.

Later bricks and tiles were made from local clay. Some buildings were made with walls of slabs split from the strong local hardwood. They were caulked and then white-washed with pipe clay, which was readily available.

In 1792 Sydney Town was reported as having '700 comfortable huts, exclusive of brick buildings, the property of the Government'.

The sandy soil around Sydney proved unsuitable for agriculture so the colony spread westwards to Parramatta and then on to the fertile river flats of the Hawkesbury. Grants of land were made to selected citizens, who were assigned a number of convicts for labour but who also needed to be housed and fed.

Many of these landholders, especially the Cox family, built substantial mansions, mostly of stone. They used the artisans among the convicts as well as tradesmen from the free migrants.

Some tools were brought out with the First Fleet, most of them only suitable for rough work, and skilled tradesmen were few. Speed of erection was the vital factor in providing shelter so axes, saws, a hammer, canthook, auger and spokeshave were the basic implements.

The real pioneering began when settlement spread into and beyond the Blue Mountains and the Great Dividing Range after Blaxland, Lawson and Wentworth discovered a way across the rugged mountains in 1813. It was then that individual settlers began carving farms out of the virgin bush. Their first task was to provide themselves with shelter and most of their dwellings were primitive indeed.

Few had any building skills or experience. Tools were few, often only an axe. Very little equipment could be transported over the rough and precipitous mountain tracks. Some of the early settlers were escaped convicts and these, in particular, were unable or unwilling to restrict their progress by carrying heavy equipment.

There was little to learn from the Aborigines. The Australian natives did not have the Europeans' obsession for acquiring possessions. They were also nomadic so their only need was shelter for their own bodies.

Timber slabs, mostly vertical but occasionally horizontal between posts, hand-made bricks laid in clay, stone (rarely dressed), saplings driven into the ground a few centimetres apart, with smaller branches laced horizontally and the whole plastered with clay or mud (often mixed with sticks, grass, cow manure), rammed earth — there seemed no limit to the ingenuity of the early pioneers in their use of building materials.

The houses were rarely designed. They grew, as quickly as possible, from the primitive materials that were at hand. Yet sometimes they achieved pleasant proportions and a sense of harmony with the environment that is sadly lacking in most of the project builders' brick boxes that have succeeded them.

The story of a first settlement on the coast, followed by expansion into the interior, although without the difficulties presented by the Blue Mountains, was repeated in what are now the other States.

The first recorded landing on Tasmanian soil took place in 1642 when the carpenter from Abel Tasman's ship swam ashore at Forestier Peninsula on the east coast. He planted the Dutch flag, claiming the island for the Netherlands (Holland). Tasman named it Van Diemen's Land.

Between 1772 and 1803 10 exploring expeditions claimed landings. It was not until the latter year, though, that the British authorities, fearing that the French were interested, made a serious attempt to settle the island.

Van Diemen's Land was thought to be part of the mainland until Bass and Flinders established it as a separate island in 1798.

The island was granted its own government in 1856 and the name officially changed to Tasmania, although this name had been in general use for some years.

The blackest page in Australia's history was the systematic and complete murder of the Aboriginal population of Tasmania. One of the results was the ignoring of Aboriginal place

Early stonework was mostly laid as rubble, but, in Tasmania especially, good stone was readily to hand and there were some tradesmen among the convicts. Stoneworking tools such as mallets, mauls, bolsters, gads, wedges, combs and stone picks were all employed.

names so that almost every town, village, river and landmark bears a British or European name.

Being a penal settlement from the beginning, there was an abundance of convict labour. There was also plenty of good building stone so that this material features largely in early buildings.

Queensland was originally part of New South Wales, as was all the east coast of Australia and New Zealand. It was opened up by expeditions from the south by both land and sea. Brisbane, first named Edinglassie (a contraction of Edinborough and Glasgow), was proclaimed a penal settlement on 15 August 1826. Queensland became a separate colony in 1859.

The western coast of Australia, at that time known as New Holland, had been sighted many times as far back as the sixteenth century. It is possible a Portuguese, Captain Meneses, went ashore in 1527. Dutch mariners recorded many sightings in the west and the north over the next 100 years. In 1642 Abel Tasman was sent to discover the extent of the Great South Land. He sailed down the west coast on his way to Van Diemen's Land (now Tasmania).

The first Englishman credited with discovering the west coast was William Dampier in the *Cygnet*, who sailed into King Sound in 1688 and stayed there for nine weeks.

A French ship was reported in the vicinity in 1772, a British in 1791 and when further French vessels showed interest the British government became suspicious. In 1826 Governor Darling was instructed to claim the territory for England. This was achieved by a small detachment of troops and convicts on 26 December 1826, when they hoisted a flag at the foot of Mount Clarence and proclaimed the Swan River Colony.

Settlement at Melbourne, known at first as the Port Phillip district of New South Wales, was not as straightforward as the others. There were several abortive attempts from 1803 onwards. In November 1834 Edward Henty settled at Portland Bay but the real foundation of the colony was laid by John Batman. In 1835 he crossed from Tasmania and 'bought', from an unsuspecting Aboriginal tribe, 600,000 acres (240,000 hectares) at the head of Port Phillip Bay.

Later in the same year another party from Tasmania landed at Westernport. They moved on to Port Phillip and sailed a short distance up the Yarra River. Here they built two turf huts — the beginning of the city of Melbourne.

In July 1836, two English ships sailed into the mouth of St Vincent's Gulf, South Australia, landing troops on Kangaroo Island. The entire island continent was finally claimed for England.

It is generally accepted that a Dutch ship sighted Arnhem Land in 1623. William Dampier was the first Englishman to make a landfall — in 1688 — but several other sightings had been made in the intervening years. Formal possession of the north coast of New Holland (now Australia) was taken in 1824 by a party sent from Port Jackson.

Settlement was moved from place to place for several reasons and it was not until 1868 that Darwin, then called Palmerston, was selected as the site of the principal town. In the meantime, in 1863, the British had declared the Northern Territory part of South Australia. It remained so until 1909 when it was taken over by the Commonwealth Government.

It is highly probable that there was sporadic Chinese settlement in the Northern Territory during this period and even before the first Dutch sightings. Recent landings by 'boat people' from Vietnam lend some credence to this theory.

Understandably, the first migrants built, as far as they could, dwellings similar to those they had left. The first houses had only one room like the small farmhouses and crofters' dwellings of England, although, on account of structural difficulties, they were usually built without the loft or attic room of the old country. There was usually one door and one window.

While this made for a cosy home in a cold climate, it was soon found unbearably hot in the temperate climate of the new land. The first concession to the environment was the addition of a veranda — a name derived from the Spanish *varanda* — on the western side and later on other sides as well.

An earth floor was all that could usually be given to the single room and was standard for verandas.

Roofing a single room was comparatively easy with a simple gable being sufficient and structurally sound. A further room could be added to one or both ends of the original building without much trouble. When it came to putting another room or rooms at the back, which was the usual and almost inevitable addition, a lean-to was the only practical solution to the problem.

Even in Europe roofs spanning more than one room were quite rare. The larger buildings were usually covered with a number of parallel gables with box gutters between.

When the roofing material was bark, or on rare occasions thatch, this method was quite impractical. This is one reason why many of the original roofs were re-covered with corrugated galvanised iron when new building materials were imported from England in sufficient quantity.

After the pioneer had provided himself with a shelter, he began to think of farming equipment. One of his first requirements was a grindstone, essential for sharpening axes and a variety of other tools. It was ingeniously set up over a trough containing water so that the surface of the stone was always damp. Next came a dray, more robust than the spring cart of England, drawn by one horse and capable of carrying loads over rough ground.

Before European Settlement

For some 30,000 to 40,000 years or more before Australia was discovered by Europeans, Aborigines roamed the continent. They lived on the land and off it with much greater understanding and much less despoliation of it than white man has managed in the short space of 200 years.

As nomadic hunters, their journeys were dictated mainly by the movement of the animals that were their main food source. They required little in the way of shelter and were indeed seldom in one place long enough to warrant the erection of permanent structures.

There were caves in some parts of the country, but these were not used to any great extent. The main building material was bark stripped from trees, in some cases in pieces up to four metres long and almost as wide. It was almost always readily to hand.

In a dry country shelter from above was rarely required and for the most part a wind break was all that was needed for a comfortable night. Anticipating with great accuracy the direction of the night wind, the Aborigines would erect a metre-high break of boughs, bark and bushes. They would gather a few green branches, twigs and grass for a bed.

When a more permanent shelter was required a framework of light saplings supported on forked sticks was sufficient to carry roof and walls of bark.

Sometimes all that was used was a sheet of bark leant against a tree trunk and held in position with one or two saplings or laced with vines.

Communal fires were practically unknown, so there were no fireplaces as we know them. Again anticipating the wind direction, each family, or sometimes even each individual, would have a small cooking fire immediately outside their hut.

The early white migrants apparently made no attempt to understand the Aborigines. The surviving written material of the day makes it plain that the natives were regarded as ignorant savages with no rights whatever.

It was not conceded that they might have a culture of their own, a strict code of morals and a way of life much more suited to the harsh country than that of the newcomers.

The Aborigines hunted for food, taking no more than was necessary. The white people — authorities, soldiers, free settlers and convicts alike — shot everything that moved, felled the trees that sheltered birds and animals and cleared the scrub that gave ground cover. Deprived of their natural food and believing that all things should be shared, it was inevitable that the Aborigines should take a sheep or a calf when they were hungry. The retaliation that followed sowed the seed for an animosity that grew into little less than open warfare.

The Aborigines could have done much to help the newcomers, who took from 1788 to 1813 with many abortive expeditions to find a way over the Blue Mountains and the Great Dividing Range, barriers that the natives had been crossing for thousands of years. In exploration, at least, a reasonable and friendly attitude to the natives would have re-written the history of Australia.

Some of the early pioneers, notable among them Dr Charles Throsby, did befriend the Aborigines and accept their help, but this attitude was frowned on by the Governor and those in authority.

When shelter more permanent than a wind break was required, a framework of light saplings supported on forked sticks was sufficient to carry roof and walls of bark and brush.

New South Wales

Australia's Oldest Church

EBENEZER,
New South Wales

1807

When the sailing ship *Coromandel*, of 500 tons, carrying 200 prisoners and a small group of free settlers, reached Port Jackson on 13 June 1802, the Colony was suffering greatly from an inadequate food supply.

The soil around Sydney Town proved poor and incapable of producing sufficient to feed the town's population. The settlers who had ventured as far as Rose Hill (now Parramatta) were little better off.

Among the *Coromandel*'s free immigrants were a dozen or so families from the English/Scottish border country. They were offered 100 acres (40 hectares) each on the banks of the Hawkesbury River, most with a river frontage.

Described as 'small farmers, sailors, artisans or shop-keepers', with little or no money, but a determination to make good, they carved productive farms and orchards out of the bush. Many of the holdings are still worked today by direct descendants of the original families.

Mostly Presbyterians, these people were pious as well as industrious so it is not surprising that they felt the need for a place of worship. They began holding meetings under a large tree and then in some of the houses. In 1803 a split slab building thatched with grass was erected on a plateau at Portland Head.

Four years later work began on a stone building designed by Andrew Johnston, an architect from Berwick-on-Tweed, who was one of the immigrants. It took two years to build and cost £400. Some settlers contributed their labour, others the proceeds of the sale of farm produce. The 60 centimetre thick walls are of local stone brought from a nearby quarry by bullock team and boat. Much of the timber was fashioned from trees felled nearby.

The congregation came through the bush on foot, in drays and a few in sulkies. Many came up or down the river in boats. For many years funeral processions by boat were a tradition.

Small boats can navigate the Hawkesbury from the sea to Windsor. This was the chief means of transport in those early days and it continued to be so for a long time until trafficable roads were formed.

It was originally intended that the new building be both church and school so a partition divided it into two sections. This accounts for the irregular spacing of the windows — the wider stonework in the centre marks the location of the partition.

A charming stone cottage was built close by as a residence for the school master. Its design was also the work of Andrew Johnston, as were several other houses in the district.

After a while some of the people feared for the safety of their children on the twice-daily walk through the bush to the school. Dangers, real or imagined, were bushrangers, Aborigines and snakes. Arrangements were made for the children to sleep at the school during the week. A staging was erected to form a loft in the school half of the building. Approached by a ladder, this was where the boys slept, while the girls were accommodated on the upper floor of the master's house.

So the Ebenezer church is not only the oldest church in Australia still in use, it was also the first boarding school.

Australia's Oldest Church

EBENEZER (1807)

Split Slab Dwelling

AGNES BANKS,
New South Wales

c. 1820

Although most of the credit for the development of the Hawkesbury District in New South Wales goes to Governor Lachlan Macquarie (1810-1821), its potential was recognised much earlier by Governor Arthur Phillip.

Governor Phillip led an expedition from Sydney Town in 1789 in search of good farming land. It was realised that the soil around Port Jackson was not productive enough to support the new colony. The party trekked through virgin bush from Manly to Broken Bay and then rowed their way up the Hawkesbury River to the area now known as Richmond.

Phillip decided that the land there was suitable for food production and recommended it be made available for vegetable growing. It was his successor, Lieutenant-Governor Francis Grose, who sent 22 settlers to the district, then known as Green Hills, to commence farming.

But development of the area really began after 1810, when Governor Macquarie made his celebrated journey and named five towns — Windsor, Richmond, Castlereagh, Pitt Town and Wilberforce — now called the 'five Macquarie towns'.

Agnes Banks is a small village near Castlereagh, the southernmost of the five towns. The slab house, pictured, is on the edge of Yarramundi Lagoon, in an area frequently flooded. Its early history appears lost, although the house was occupied more recently, before being abandoned, by a Macedonian family.

Built mainly of vertically placed split slabs, it differs from the usual construction in that although the slabs are set into the bottom plate, the top plate is placed on the inside of the slabs and spiked to them.

There are round log ceiling joists placed 750 millimetres apart, the rafters are saplings and sawn battens cross them to take the split oak shingles.

There is a fireplace of hand-made bricks at the western end. This again is unusual as the brickwork is continued for the full length of the end wall.

Although one of Macquarie's conditions for the grant of farming land at Green Hills was that dwellings and towns were to be built above flood level, many of the farm buildings have been inundated many times.

The result is considerable immediate loss, many hazardous rescue operations and much heartache, but eventually the land is further improved by another deposit of rich topsoil from further up the river. The worst flood recorded was in 1867 when the river rose 19 metres above its normal level. Even minor floods leave debris among tree branches several metres above ground level.

RASmolicz '82

Split Slab Dwelling

AGNES BANKS (c. 1820)

Shepherd's Hut

CALALA STATION,

New South Wales

1830

When Philip Gidley King, grandson of the third governor of New South Wales, was made manager of the Peel River Company's estates on the Liverpool Plains in northern New South Wales, he had an imposing brick homestead built at Calala. The area is now part of the city of Tamworth. Already on the estate and in close proximity to the new building was the shepherd's hut pictured here.

Dating back to 1830, the hut is typical of the slab huts of the period. Tools were scarce and building materials were only those at hand, often the trees cut down to clear a space for the dwelling.

It is one of the earliest examples of a house with a veranda, but it is unusual in that the veranda is on the southern side, providing no shade at all. There are two rooms under the main roof, with two more under a lean-to on the northern side.

Walls are of split slabs placed vertically, the spaces between filled with a mixture of sand and mud. The inside walls are covered with newspapers. The original wooden shutters were at some stage replaced with glazed windows.

The wooden floor is practically on the ground, following the practice in England where termites were unknown.

The wide fireplace of hand-made bricks was used for cooking and heating. Cooking pots and billy cans would have been suspended on wires from a set-in iron bar.

The roof is covered with bark laid over sapling frames, originally laced with vines or wire. More saplings were overlaid to hold the bark in place.

The saplings of the over-frame were drilled at the intersections to take whittled pegs. These were used as connectors. Saplings running up the roof were carried beyond the ridge and wooden pegs again were used to connect the overlapping saplings.

One of the two main rooms was used for living, eating and cooking, the other for sleeping. The smaller rooms under the lean-to were used for storing food and equipment.

The Calala shepherd's hut is still standing and is being maintained by the Tamworth Historical Society.

Shepherd's Hut

CALALA STATION (1830)

Bushranger's House

CARCOAR,
New South Wales

1840s

Thomas Icely settled in the beautiful Carcoar district in 1840, joining earlier settlers who had taken up land without official blessing. But the peace and tranquillity of the lovely valley was soon to be threatened by what Icely described as 'unruly convicts and bushrangers'.

A butcher's apprentice known as Frank Gardiner decided that bushranging would be a more exciting and possibly more rewarding trade and laid down his knife and cleaver. The shop in which he worked can still be seen in Icely Street, Carcoar.

Gardiner teamed up with John Piesley, another ticket-of-leave man from Bathurst. Together they held up coaches on the Bathurst to Lambing Flat run until Piesley was caught and hanged in 1862.

Gardiner was then joined by John O'Meally and Johnny Gilbert. The trio made history in 1863 with an attempt to hold up the local branch of the Commercial Banking Company of Sydney. The escapade was unsuccessful, but the bushrangers escaped.

Other rascals were attracted to the gang, the best known among them Ben Hall. Hall knew the district well. He was born at Breeza in the north-west of New South Wales and then leased a farm near Wheogo in the Grenfell area, in 1852, when about 16 years of age. He gained a reputation as a good and hard worker. During this period he developed a friendship with 'Flash' Dan Charters who lived in the hut pictured, a little more than a kilometre from the waters now backed up by the Carcoar Dam.

When, in 1856, the birth of his child was imminent, Hall brought his wife the considerable distance to Dan's dwelling where their son was born.

Six years later, on 15 June 1862, Gardiner's gang made their most successful raid. It became known as the Eugowra Escort Raid and the haul was £12,000 worth of coin and gold dust.

Immediately Hall's peaceful life as a farmer ended. His wife deserted him and he was charged with complicity in the Eugowra robbery. The charge was dismissed, but the proceedings took four months. When he returned to his farm he found his stock had either strayed or died.

It is fairly certain he was concerned in the raid. A few weeks later he was found by police in the company of one of Gardiner's gang and the two men were chased and fired on. Hall then joined the gang. Gardiner had disappeared immediately after the Eugowra Raid but Hall and Gilbert carried on in the area for another three years.

Dan Charters' cottage is on the property of Mr S. Johns and is very much in its original condition, although corrugated galvanised iron now covers the gable ends and the shingles of the roof.

The walls generally are of split slabs, placed vertically and nailed to top and bottom plates on the inside. There is a brick chimney at one end in a wall of stone in random rubble. There is certain to have always been a fireplace in this wall but the brick fireplace and chimney may have been a later improvement.

The structure, generally, is a little more substantial than was typical of the period. It has endured and is still occupied.

Bushranger's House

CARCOAR (1840s)

Pioneer Farmhouse

NATTAI RIVER,
New South Wales

c. 1840

Primitive ploughs, some of them home made, were used to break up the ground. From these developed the single and double furrow mouldboards still in use on small holdings. The harrows, often weighted with rocks or logs, were used to break up the clods.

The Nattai River rises near Mittagong and flows through rugged hilly and later mountainous country to join the Wollondilly River. Here the road from Camden to the silver-mining town of Yerranderie once crossed the Nattai before the Warragamba Dam flooded the valley and formed Lake Burragorang.

A few hardy settlers established themselves in this secluded valley very early in the Colony's history, probably because it *was* secluded and in those days practically inaccessible.

Typical of their dwellings is that pictured here which is now submerged under the waters of Lake Burragorang. Walls were of vertical slabs split from the trees that were felled to make space for it and trenched into bottom and top plates of rough-hewn logs.

The roof was a simple gable with rafters of slightly lighter logs. There was no ceiling but here and there a beam spanned the rooms to prevent the walls from spreading. A cross wall that divided the structure into two rooms also had a stabilising effect.

Roof and gable ends were covered with bark then attached to framing at the ends and to saplings secured across the rafters. They were further secured by more saplings placed over them and wired or pegged into position.

The fireplace, wide enough to serve for heating as well as cooking, was built within a separate structure. It was framed with angle posts, into which slabs were dropped horizontally. The fireplace was capped from the eaves level with a galvanised iron gathering and chimney stalk.

The fireplace proper was lined inside with stone set in clay and lavishly plastered. This must have needed constant renewal.

The house and an area around it large enough for a few fruit trees and a vegetable garden was enclosed within a palisade of logs driven into the ground and butting against each other. Longer logs, pegged on or spiked, served as a rail near the top. When fencing wire was available this was used to lace the rail to the vertical logs.

Pioneer Farmhouse

NATTAI RIVER (c. 1840)

O'Brien's Farmhouse

LITTLE RIVER,
New South Wales

c. 1840

Some types of Casuarina trees (river oaks, sheoaks, swamp oaks) were suitable for shingles. The froe, a fairly long blade with a wooden handle, was held over the sawn log and driven in with a mallet, splitting the timber with comparative ease.

Very early in the history of the colony, several small farms were established on the banks of the Nattai River and its tributary, the Little River. The first dwellings featured split slab walls with a bark roof covering but construction became more sophisticated as skills were developed and imported materials became available.

O'Brien's farmhouse, pictured, on the banks of the Little River showed some advance on most of the pioneer dwellings remaining in the area.

Walls were framed with roughly squared bottom and top plates and posts tenoned into them at about one metre intervals. The posts were grooved so that wall slabs could be dropped horizontally between them. In some places battens were secured to the posts, both inside and out, to hold the slabs in place, thus eliminating the laborious grooving of posts.

O'Brien's house was originally roofed with bark, but this was later replaced with corrugated galvanised iron. When iron became available it was usually placed straight over a shingled roof, but with a roofing of bark the original covering was removed.

This was a rather pretentious four-roomed house, boasting two fireplaces. These were lined with stones laid in clay and sheathed with vertical timber slabs. Galvanised iron was used in a crude gathering that led into the chimney stalk.

Chinks between slabs were filled with a plaster made of river clay and grass. The same material was used to smooth the inside wall surfaces. Newspaper was used as a wallpaper and to retain the crude plaster. Dates on these newspapers, where still legible, suggest that the wallpaper was often refurbished.

The first settlers in these remote places were barely self-supporting for, apart from bartering amongst themselves, there was no outlet for their produce.

The tracks between them were gradually extended, often by stray cattle, and finally provided reasonable access to the larger townships. Farm produce and cattle could then be taken to towns like Mittagong and Camden and, by way of the Burragorang Valley, to Wentworth Falls.

Many of the original dwellings and farms in this area are now under the waters of the Burragorang Dam.

O'Brien's Farmhouse

LITTLE RIVER (c. 1840)

Pioneer Cottage

MEGALONG VALLEY,
New South Wales

c. 1850

The area now known as the Blue Mountains to the west of Sydney was called Carmarthen and Lansdowne Hills by Governor Phillip in 1788. These names were soon dropped in favour of the present more popular and descriptive one. The familiar blue haze of distance is accentuated by the effect of the sun's rays on the oil given off by the eucalyptus trees which are abundant in the area.

One of the earliest valleys to be settled was Megalong, surveyed in 1838. This was well ahead of most of the mountain towns, including the most well known, Katoomba. Access is difficult and the valley is usually approached by a track down the steep mountain side from Blackheath. Small farms were established by people who, for various reasons, preferred the quiet and seclusion of the valley. They shared it with members of the Daruk tribe of Aborigines.

The major portion of one of the valley's earliest dwellings still stands just off the main road, not far from the post office. Its walls are 200 millimetres thick, made of a mixture of sand and gravel. The mixture appears to have been rammed into position between some kind of forming, probably like an early type of pisé.

There is a projecting gabled room at each end, while the centre section has a ridged roof running across the building. A veranda links the two end wings.

In the middle of the centre section, at the front and back, is a stout, round post. Another post on each side frames the door openings. A log of similar diameter extends the full length

of each wall, combining door heads with a continuous plate. Without this the walls probably would not have been able to support the roof, which is built with sapling rafters. Smaller saplings were laid across them to provide support and fastening for the bark covering.

At the junction of the main road and another that leads to the adjoining Kanimbla Valley, there is a church whose story is a potted version of the trials and spirit of the valley dwellers.

The first church on the site was a small wattle and daub structure built in 1901. In the course of his duties the minister, the Rev F. V. Pratt, who was stationed at Katoomba, walked all over the surrounding country and as far afield as the Burragorang Valley.

The wattle and daub church was destroyed by fire in 1905.

Fifteen years later the teacher from the valley school, which is opposite the road junction, was instrumental in having services renewed. They were held in houses at first and then in a new pisé church built by volunteer labour. This became unsafe and was demolished in 1942.

The present church was built in 1943 and stands in a memorial garden of native shrubs and trees. Mounted near the church steps is a stone that was used by the Aborigines for sharpening tools.

When this painting was made the cottage was in an advanced stage of dilapidation, but there was evidence that some sort of restoration work was contemplated.

Pioneer Cottage

MEGALONG VALLEY (c. 1850)

Church

CAPERTEE,

New South Wales

c. 1850

The churches played an important part in the lives of the early settlers. Possibly influenced in some degree by the European practice of building a village around a church, small communities soon had a modest place of worship under construction. It was usually extremely simple in design and its cost negligible as most of the materials were donated and the labour voluntary.

Primarily intended for church services, the building doubled as a meeting place, the venue for any community function and in some instances as a school.

When the First Fleet was being assembled in England a student was found who was willing to accompany it as chaplain. He was hurriedly ordained and so Richard Johnson arrived in the colony as the first minister of religion. His first service in the new land was held under a tree, probably in what is now Macquarie Place.

Congregationalists were represented here quite early, sent by the London Missionary Society and the Colonial Missionary Society. Their first preacher is reported as being at Parramatta in 1798. Later, missionaries came from Tahiti and in 1810 one named Crook organised the first Congregationalist church at the corner of Bligh and Castlereagh Streets.

The first Presbyterian free settlers were the group of Scots who settled at Portland Head on the Hawkesbury River in 1802. They included among their number a James Mein, an elder from London. He conducted services in houses and the open air until Ebenezer church was built.

There were several early Baptist gatherings before a fully accredited minister, Pastor McCabe, preached in a room of the Rose and Crown Inn in Castlereagh Street in 1831.

For 36 years efforts to send Roman Catholic priests to the colony were frustrated by the English Government and it was not until 1819 that New Holland was included in the Parish of Cape of Good Hope.

As the pioneers moved further out into the country the various churches followed. In general the English migrants were inclined to remain in the towns, while the Irish played the major part in opening up the country. In consequence the majority of early churches in the outback areas are Roman Catholic.

This church not far from the town of Capertee nestles comfortably in its setting of native trees. The walls are of richly coloured stone laid as random rubble, necessitating liberal quantities of mortar and presenting a rich colour pageant as they reflect the afternoon sunlight. They are capped with a corrugated roof over the original shingles.

A large lancet head window, well proportioned and with dressed reveals and sill, adds character to the end wall, while smaller windows are symmetrically placed on the front and rear walls.

The bell tower which straddles the roof is quite decorative with a simple use of timber members. It has a pyramidal capping, surmounted with a small orb and a cross.

Capertee, once a centre of coal and shale mining, has now diminished in importance, but still serves a pastoral community.

Church

CAPERTEE (c. 1850)

Brick Dwelling

CARCOAR,
New South Wales

c. 1850

Decorative panels are a feature of the wall over the veranda on the street front. The panels at each end are recessed, the centre one projecting. The different coloured bricks are mottled on the straight walls.

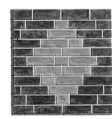

The historic town of Carcoar is built in a valley with steep hills on all sides, as was the custom in early New South Wales. This was distinct from early European towns and villages which invariably occupied hilltop sites as a protection against invaders. Proximity to water was the prime consideration here.

Pioneer settlers followed close on the heels of the exploring party led by Blaxland, Wentworth and Lawson in 1813. The surveyor, George William Evans, who explored much of the central west, is reported as having camped at Coombing Creek, near Carcoar, in 1815.

By 1820 settlers were moving into the area. The first grant of land was 560 acres (224 hectares) to Thomas Icely in 1840. He named his property 'Coombing'. It is still known by that name.

When the area was first mapped the draughtsmen called it variously Carcuan, Corcoran and finally Carcoar.

By 1850 Carcoar was the second most populous town west of the Blue Mountains. From that time many fine examples of nineteenth century buildings were erected, starting with the police station and barracks.

Icely discovered gold in the district and between 1876 and 1881 30,000 ounces (850.5 kg) were recovered. The population rose to 600, but the discovery of richer deposits further west took many of the men away and the population steadily declined. It is now 400.

The early Carcoar dwelling pictured is unique in many ways, one being its location on a hilltop overlooking the town proper.

It is unique also in the extensive use of brick in both a structural and decorative manner. There was a brickworks nearby and it is possible this house was built for the brickmaster.

Whilst there is a veranda on three sides, in deference to the colony's climate, the house features a fairly steep pitched roof in which three bedrooms are accommodated. English customs obviously still had a strong influence on the thinking of the settlers. There is a window in each gable end and a dormer window at the rear to light the centre room.

The front brick wall, built in a variation of Flemish bond, continues up beyond the veranda roof and features three decorative panels. The centred entrance door is surmounted by a semi-circular fanlight of excellent design, contained within a brick arch. Part of this arch is intersected by the veranda roof, suggesting that the veranda was an afterthought.

The veranda at the entrance is paved with 175 millimetre square bricks laid diagonally. Regular bricks are used to pave the side and rear verandas. Octagonal brick chimneys are another striking feature.

Veranda posts are distinguished by brackets featuring a Greek motif and suspended from the veranda plates are decorative galvanised iron cutouts. Similar cutouts, but of a different design, are suspended from the eaves fascia and are, indeed, a feature of several other Carcoar buildings.

The house is currently occupied by the Stammers family.

Brick Dwelling

CARCOAR (c. 1850)

Miner's Hut

STUART TOWN,
New South Wales

c. 1855

Fossickers equipped themselves with those mining tools they could afford, but gave little thought to house-building tools. An axe was often all they had for the job that followed a lucky strike.

Much of the history of the colony of New South Wales has been poorly recorded or not recorded at all and many of the accepted circumstances are open to doubt. Among these is the official version of the discovery of gold.

There is still in existence a field book of a surveyor, James McBrien, in which he records finding gold between Rydal and Bathurst, in western New South Wales, in 1823. Further discoveries were made near Hartley, 1839, the head of the Cox River, 1841, the Wollondilly, 1842, and by a shepherd named Macgregor near Stuart Town in 1843. News of these finds was suppressed by the Governor, Sir George Gipps, who feared the consequences of a gold rush in such a sparsely populated colony, with only a small law-keeping force.

When it became impossible to suppress the knowledge any longer, gold found at Ophir, near Bathurst, in 1851 by two prospectors, Lister and Tod, was naively entrusted to one E. H. Hargraves. He showed it to the Governor, claimed he had discovered it, was given a reward and appears in the history books as the discoverer of gold in Australia.

The release of this news triggered the inevitable rush. The population of New South Wales rose from 77,345 in 1851 to 231,925 in 1854 and 410,766 in 1857. Towns near the finds mushroomed almost overnight, with tents as the first dwellings, followed by huts of the most primitive and original construction.

The six metre by four metre hut pictured, at Stuart Town, is typical. The construction illustrated either a lack of skill or suitable tools. Most of the early pioneer homes were constructed of split slabs, either used vertically or set horizontally in a frame, whereas here whole logs were used, merely placed one above the other.

In orthodox log cabin construction the logs are lapped and cogged together at the corners. In this hut only the logs of the long walls were extended and those of the shorter end walls were merely butted into them. A post set in the ground at the angle formed, and extending the full height of the walls, provided the stability otherwise lacking. It also held the stack of logs in place. Fencing wire was used to tie logs and posts together.

More log posts were used at strategic points on each side of the door opening on the long walls and in the centre of the end walls. The walls were lined inside with hessian.

Roof framing was the typical sapling construction of rafters with lighter saplings laid across them. Sheets of bark were then secured to the saplings with vines or wire. Matching holes were pierced in the lapping bark sheets in order to lace them together. Then saplings were laid over the top to make the covering more secure. It was effective, if inelegant.

There is the usual fireplace. Here it was made with small sheets of flat galvanised iron, plastered over on the outside with mud laid over chicken wire. Earth floors were typical.

No provision was made for catching rain water. There was no real need as the miners, like most of the early pioneers, sited their dwellings close to a creek.

The hut, though still standing, has not been occupied for some considerable time.

Miner's Hut

STUART TOWN (c. 1855)

Early Cottage

LYNDHURST,
New South Wales

c. 1860

All goldfields were first distinguished by a conglomeration of multi-shaped and -coloured tents. They were erected without any regard to symmetry and unhampered by the rigid town planning regulations which now tend to make life more difficult.

When the fields proved successful, even for only a short period, tents were replaced by shacks or huts. They were erected as quickly as possible but provided shelter in some degree more substantial than canvas.

Later, when a certain measure of permanency seemed assured, additions, often quite incongruous, were made.

The Bathurst district was perhaps the richest gold mining area in New South Wales. The field spread out, covering a large amount of country, with Bathurst as its centre. The town of Lyndhurst was near the southern perimeter.

Pictured is an abandoned dwelling not far from Lyndhurst. It was obviously built in two parts, although it is impossible to tell which was the first.

Nearest the roadway is a two-roomed section with walls of vertical split slabs. It is roofed with corrugated galvanised iron and has a veranda, probably not original. The massive dual purpose (cooking and heating) fireplace is built in rich russet-coloured, hand-made bricks. With its outsize chimney it dominates the little dwelling.

At the rear there is almost a separate structure, built in a quite different way. Some of the walls are vertical split slabs but most are split logs laid horizontally, reminiscent of the log cabins of central Europe and Canada.

The fireplace is stone laid in clay, with a split timber backing. It gathers over and continues as a chimney of corrugated galvanised iron.

The English-made iron imported for these buildings was heavily galvanised and a life of 100 to 150 years, especially in the dry atmosphere of outback Australia, was not uncommon.

When the gold was worked out, Lyndhurst, like most of the gold-mining towns, lost its importance although it still serves a grazing community. Recently the Olympic Way was diverted to bypass the town.

Early Cottage

LYNDHURST (NEAR BATHURST) (c. 1860)

Uniting Church

ILFORD,
New South Wales

1866

Originally known as Cain's or Keen's Swamp, Ilford is a small town in the Rylstone-Kandos area of New South Wales, not far from Bathurst.

In 1837 Thomas Harris brought his family from Wiltshire in England to this then remote place. Twelve years later Reubin Leader came from Essex to take up adjoining land. Both families were devout and missed, no doubt among other things, regular Sunday worship.

For some years the Methodist minister from Mudgee travelled to Keen's Swamp once every three months to hold a service in Reubin Leader's home. Feeling that this arrangement was still inadequate, the two families joined forces and agreed to finance the building of a local chapel. In 1866 William Harris, a son of the original Thomas Harris, donated some land facing what was then the main road to Rylstone, and an apparently unmarked foundation stone was laid in the same year.

George Harris, another son, entered into a contract to build the church for the sum of £240 and gave his labour as a carpenter free. William Harris was an unpaid stonemason, working with two other paid masons.

The stone came from a quarry east of Keen's Swamp. The cedar for the fixtures and furnishings was felled and dressed at nearby Nullo Mountain and brought to the site by bullock team.

Designed by a Sydney architect named Rowe, the building features immaculate ashlar stonework, still in excellent condition. This was possibly because the original workmanship was much better than was normal for the period. The stone is sparrow picked on the face, with chisel-draughted margins to quoin stones.

The door and window openings are lancet arched. The label mould over the door opening is unique in that it is simplified into an arrowhead shape instead of following the line of the arch. The test of time has proved this departure from style is effective.

Window reveals are splayed both inside and out. The internal finish of the walls was originally smooth-worked stone. The corner bell tower, slender and graceful, is a striking feature.

Keen's Swamp was later renamed Ilford after Reubin Leader's English birthplace and from a small beginning it grew into an important crossroads town. It became a way-station for the coaching service and this brought the inevitable inns, hotels, boarding houses, police station and lock-up, school, shops and some of the less savoury aspects of frontier towns of the early days.

Change came with the railway in 1884. Better transport meant much of the significance of the pioneer coaching towns was lost and Ilford slipped back to its earlier quiet. While still a centre of farming activities, it retains much of its early charm.

The church served its purpose without any major maintenance for 100 years. Then in preparation for the centenary celebrations, restorative maintenance was carried out.

Despite some modernisation, the spirit of the original church has remained.

RA Smolicz '81.

Uniting Church

ILFORD (1866)

Railway Cottage

BLUE MOUNTAINS,
New South Wales

1867

A number of stone cottages were built in the mid 1800s alongside the railway line between Emu Plains and Mount Victoria and are now known locally as 'Railway Houses'. Sited where the western road crossed the line, they were occupied by gatekeepers.

There were seven crossings but only six of them had gatekeeper's cottages.

Built to a standard plan, the cottages have a distinctive charm. They have a feeling for the environment with a sensitive use of natural and readily available materials.

The first was built at Emu Plains in 1867, but, except for the sandstone walls, was destroyed during the 1968 bushfire.

The plan of the cottages is compact and economical, but the outside appearance seems to have been the designer's first consideration.

There is a central living room, with a bedroom on each side and kitchen behind. The steep roof is gabled. In some houses there are four gables whereas in others there are three with the rear section as a lean-to. A porch, with its roof supported on a single post, is tucked into one of the angles of the crucifix shape. It leads directly into the living room.

The gables are enriched with attractive carved bargeboards. and the standard of the stonework is excellent.

The extension of the railway line from Penrith to Wentworth Falls was important for a number of reasons. It opened up that area of the Blue Mountains with the establishment of several towns and made travel to the west so much easier. It also provided employment at a time when the Colony badly needed such a stimulus.

The names of several of the mountain towns have been changed more than once and each carries an interesting snippet of history.

Emu, now Emu Plains, explains itself. The next up the line was Lucasville, a railway platform established because a member of parliament named Lucas lived there. Then there was Wascoe, now Blaxland, named after a prominent land owner. Later Wascoe's Siding was established between Lucasville and Wascoe, once a watering stop for the steam engines after the arduous pull up from the plains.

Eager's Siding, then Valley, now Valley Heights, owed its name to the large valley where Cobb & Co coaches rested their horses. They needed to have fresh teams to continue on after an overnight stop at Loloma, Springwood. Springwood was the site of a camp by Major Cox's road building gang, chosen because of a spring of fresh water.

Further west was Buss' Siding, named for the already well-established Buss' Inn. It later became a boarding school known as Woodford Academy. Lawson was originally called Blue Mountain and Wentworth Falls was known as Weatherboard, after The Weatherboard Inn, a well known stopping place that was established there well before the railway extension. It was within 200 metres of the present railway station.

A few of the railway cottages are still occupied, but most are in various stages of disrepair.

Railway Cottage

BLUE MOUNTAINS (1867)

Police Station

EMU PLAINS,
New South Wales

c. 1870

The Nepean River at Penrith was first crossed by a ford a little upstream from the present Victoria Bridge. Later a punt was used for crossing and a short road up to the present highway was appropriately named Punt Road. The punt was replaced by a wooden bridge, but this was washed away in a flood in 1857. A second timber bridge suffered the same fate three years later.

The first Emu Plains Police Station was built on the corner of Punt Road. The site was purchased from the Crown in 1858 for the sum of £6 and sold very soon after for £80. An Emu Plains drover, George Laing, bought it in 1878 for £400, this price suggesting that there was then a building on it. This was probably the small building that still exists, although in a poor state of repair, immediately behind the building pictured. It is a curious mixture of hand-made brick, timber framing, slab construction and lath and plaster.

It is possible, however, that the police station was built before 1878. It was certainly there when the land was bought, in 1891, by First-Class Constable William Bressington. It appears to have been used as a police station from then until 1908 when a new station and residence was built nearer the river. This is still owned by the Police Department and is rented by a retired police officer.

Many of the structural timbers used in the original police station are of a size more like those used in bridge construction than cottage work. This suggests that timber salvaged from one or both of the wrecked timber bridges was used in the building.

It was built of rough-hewn slab walls (now covered with weatherboards) and roofed with wooden shingles (later protected by corrugated galvanised iron).

Many of the shingles used on the early houses in Sydney Town were cut in Popran Valley and taken down the Hawkesbury River and on to Port Jackson by ketch. It is probable that those used on the police station were taken upstream from Popran Valley to Emu Plains.

The slab walls were covered inside with lath and plaster and later papered. Ceilings are also lath and plaster.

The floors are of sawn boards butted together, lacking the modern tongue and groove. An unusual feature of construction is that the floor joists in the main room are laid diagonally for no apparent reason. Heavy braces have been placed over the plaster finish on the walls and ceilings, suggesting this was done to correct some lateral movement. Chimneys are of hand-made bricks.

The building has been unoccupied for some time and has fallen into disrepair. However, moves are now under way to restore it.

Police Station

EMU PLAINS (c. 1870)

Early Dwelling

EMU PLAINS,
New South Wales

c. 1870

Little is known of this dwelling also situated quite close behind the old police station. With walls of hand-made bricks and originally roofed with shingles, it appears to have been built at about the same time as the police station.

Immediately behind the original police station and dwelling (previous page) at Emu Plains there stands what is probably an even older building. It is possible that the two were occupied together.

Known originally as Emu, this old settlement on the west bank of the Nepean River enjoyed a position of some importance for much of the Colony's early history. The river was named after a Secretary-of-State for the Colonies, Lord Nepean, who pronounced his name with the emphasis on the first syllable — *Nep*-ean.

Although the Blue Mountains were the great barrier against expansion to the west, the Nepean River was also a minor stumbling block. After usually three days' march, at least, from the coast, the west-bound traffic halted for a rest after crossing the river and before embarking on the major task of climbing the range. One result of this was that in its heyday Emu boasted 11 inns, the best known being the 'Arms of Australia'. It is now restored and used as an historical museum.

The building behind the old police station is fairly typical of its time. It appears to have been built in two parts. This was not unusual as the need for immediate shelter led to the quick erection of a minimum dwelling, with the intention of adding something better soon afterwards.

When it came to making the addition the original plan sometimes was unworkable and again it was a case of putting up something as quickly as possible. Often the standard of the addition was even inferior to the original, which is exactly what happened here.

The first room had walls of hand-made brick, built in the European fashion 230 millimetres thick. These soon proved not to be weathertight. In this case the remedy was an inside lining of tongue-and-grooved-and-beaded boards fixed vertically to wainscot height and then horizontally.

The walls are only 2.15 metres high and door openings 1.83 metres. The ceiling is hessian. The flooring is sawn boards, butted together. They must have been well seasoned for even after this passage of time they are surprisingly close.

There is a fireplace at the eastern end of the room.

The second room is in the form of a lean-to, framed up in timber with sawn weatherboards on the outside and lining boards on the inside. The floor is earthen, a step down from the first room to give the required height to the ceiling. This is lined with patterned pressed metal in squares, with wooden battens running the full length of the room every 600 millimetres.

This added room, which is really quite small, surprisingly has two brick fireplaces. There is one on the eastern wall and another on the south. While winter mornings at Emu Plains are often ushered in with a heavy frost, the reason for two fireplaces remains a mystery.

Both gable and lean-to portions of the roof were covered with shingles.

Unoccupied and derelict, sadly the house is now in a dilapidated condition.

Early Dwelling

EMU PLAINS (c. 1870)

Post Office, Store and Dwelling

KANGAROO VALLEY,
New South Wales

1871

The discovery of Kangaroo Valley, in 1818, is attributed to Dr Charles Throsby. It is likely, though, that the valley was sighted from Cambewarra Mountain in 1812 by the Surveyor-General, George Evans, and possibly entered by stockmen in 1817.

In 1818, Throsby was commissioned by Governor Macquarie to find a cross-country route from the settlements south of Sydney to the coast at Jervis Bay. He set out from his home at Glenfield accompanied by a surveyor James Meehan, Joseph Wild, Hamilton Hume, six convicts, two Aborigines, and a boy.

After a few days the party split up, some deciding the maze of gorges too precipitous. Throsby, Wild, the boy and the two Aborigines went on alone. They were joined by two other Aborigines, already known to Throsby, who led them down into the valley. It shows how much easier the exploration of the new land would have been if the European invaders had accepted the help of the Aborigines instead of antagonising them.

The party received further help from Timealong, the probable chief of the Wodi-wodi tribe. His forebears had inhabited the valley for thousands of years and knew numerous tracks and passes in and out of it.

After a second expedition led by Dr Throsby in 1821, European settlement slowly extended into the valley — first with cattle then for cedar-cutting.

Dairy farming was established in 1840 and has continued through many setbacks and resurgences to the present day.

Early in the valley's history the residents began pressing the authorities in Sydney for a school and a post office. Since then there have been as many as five schools in the valley, now there is one.

In 1870 Walter Arthur Nugent was appointed postmaster with a salary of £12 per annum. He was also the valley's first store-keeper. From the latter part of 1871 both functions were conducted from the building pictured here.

From the veranda the store was entered through a centre doorway. A private inner door led into the post office section at the end of the veranda. From the small window on the return wall, letters were handed out and postage stamps purchased.

The building stands on piers of stone and hand-made bricks. Solid stone steps lead onto the veranda. Framed with pit-sawn timber, the walls and roof are covered with corrugated iron. Those facing the veranda are exceptions with sawn and nosed weatherboards used.

Inside the walls are variously covered with corrugated iron placed vertically, in some cases, horizontally, and in one case with timber linings. The floors are of sawn timber without the modern tongue and grooving, providing an escape route for small coins. Ceilings are mostly hessian.

The fireplace is on a base of hand-made bricks and is sheathed on the outside with corrugated iron.

When the Kangaroo Valley Historical Society was formed in 1952 the old post office and store was its first museum, but it is now deserted and fast becoming derelict.

Post Office, Store and Dwelling

KANGAROO VALLEY (1871)

Weemala

FAULCONBRIDGE,
New South Wales

1882

The extension of the railway line in the Blue Mountains from Penrith to Wentworth Falls, then called Weatherboard, was completed in July 1867. Some eight to ten years later some of the wealthier city folk began to think of 'country homes'. The Blue Mountains were the obvious location.

Until then the buildings on the Mountains were a few slab and bark huts, built by sleeper cutters working for the railway, and wayside inns catering for coach and other travellers. Inns were fairly frequent as coaches could not travel very fast on the appalling roads.

The move to the Mountains appears to have begun with Sir Henry Parkes who acquired 500 to 600 acres (200 to 240 hectares) at Faulconbridge in 1876 in the period between his second and third terms as Premier. He built a timber house which he called Stonehurst after his native English village Stoneleigh. Three years later he built a second dwelling, now known as Faulconbridge House. The name Faulconbridge, which he gave to the village, was the maiden name of his mother, Martha.

Also in 1876, an associate of Sir Henry Parkes, Sir James Martin, Chief Justice of New South Wales and three times Premier, bought 900 acres (360 hectares) a little to the west and erected a timber cottage, alongside the railway line, which he named Numantia.

A railway station, also named Numantia, was established towards the south-western end of Sir James's property, quite close to the present-day Linden, then known as 17 Mile Hollow.

Two other associates of Parkes and Martin bought small portions of Sir James's land in late 1876. These were Sir Alfred Stephen, former Chief Justice, and Professor Charles Badham D.D. of Sydney University.

Sir Alfred built a house which he named Alphington, close to and similar to that of Sir James Martin. A stone wall was erected alongside the railway line, possibly for privacy, but it also enclosed a protected courtyard beside the house.

Sir James planned a further house, a stone mansion of 20 or more rooms and a tower, on a site from which the view 'stretched as far as Maitland and Brisbane Water'. Massive stone footings and two stone water tanks were built before the project was abandoned.

Known as Martin's Folly, these reminders of a grandiose dream remained until some time later a smaller house was built on part of the original footings.

In 1882 the Martin property was sold to Andrew H. McColluch, who had a stone house designed by G. A. Mansfield. It was constructed by a Faulconbridge stone mason and builder named Paddy Ryan. This was a short distance south of Alphington. This house was named Weemala, an Aboriginal word broadly translated as 'an expansive view'.

About this time the railway authorities established Alphington Stopping Place for the convenience of these very important landholders. It was necessary to inform the guard beforehand if there were passengers to be set down and those desiring to board the train were required to 'flag' it to a halt. As it was a

Weemala

FAULCONBRIDGE (1882)

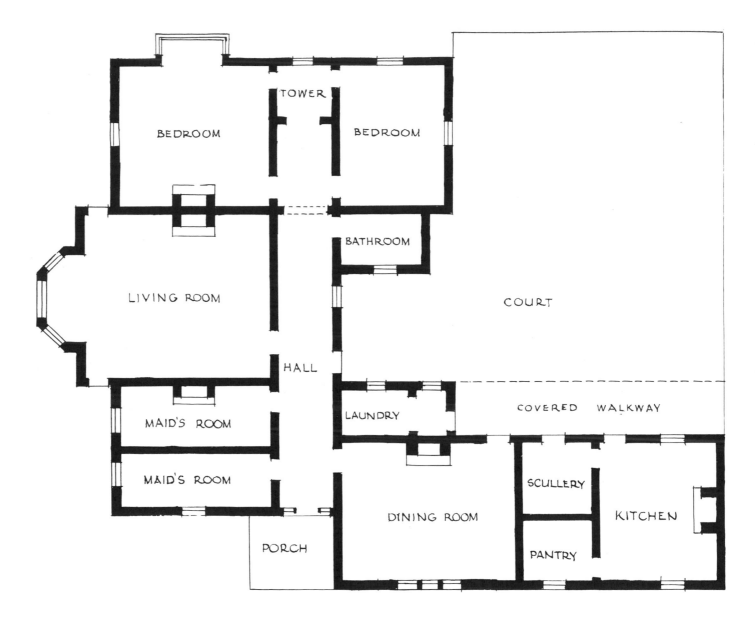

TOWER

BEDROOM

BEDROOM

BATHROOM

LIVING ROOM

COURT

HALL

MAID'S ROOM

LAUNDRY

COVERED WALKWAY

MAID'S ROOM

SCULLERY

KITCHEN

DINING ROOM

PORCH

PANTRY

The plan of Weemala is on the monumental lines of the medium-sized English mansions of the time.

Ruined hall, Weemala

Weemala tower which commanded an excellent view.

53

steep gradient here, the driver frequently had difficulty in restarting his train.

Weemala was sold during the depression of 1889, and again nine years later, this time to a solicitor named George Evans, who changed the name to Eurama, a Greek word with a similar meaning to Weemala. There were two more changes of ownership during which the house suffered from neglect and vandalism. It was also occasionally used by campers during periods of non-occupation.

Much restoration work had been done by the last owner but sadly the house was destroyed by bushfire in 1968.

The house was planned on the rather monumental lines of the medium-sized English mansions of the time. There was a central hall running the full length of the building with a large living room and three bedrooms opening on the left. A fourth bedroom and a bathroom were on the right with a door to an extensive paved court.

A wing which enclosed the second side of the court housed dining room, kitchen, scullery and pantry.

The main structural material was rock-faced stone laid in 150 millimetre courses, with large quoin stones, each two courses in height, presenting a very attractive appearance.

The quoin stones were either dressed smooth or sparrow picked. The lintels over the doors and windows and sills and hearths were all dressed stones, some quite large. The lintel stone, more than two metres long, which spanned the double entrance doors was dressed back to allow the shield in the centre to stand out in bas relief, while the motto *Viet Animo* is a fine example of the masons' art.

The stonework is still standing after the bushfire but nothing is now left of the timber floors. The roof was framed conventionally and covered with slate.

The view from the bay window of the living room and in fact from most windows must have been unsurpassed.

Some time in its checkered career the name Weemala was transferred to Numantia. Changes of name and ownership have led to considerable confusion regarding these and several other early houses in the Faulconbridge area.

Michael Chapman, a Member of Parliament and Mayor of Sydney Town, built a house, which he called Choyne Lodge, on the right hand side of Chapman Parade. When this burnt down he had a stone house built on the site, naming it, appropriately enough, Phoenix Lodge. On changing hands it was renamed Coomassie.

Chapman built another stone house across the road and this was named Knock-y-theina, but on the sale of Phoenix Lodge the name plate was retained and the second house acquired this name.

It is almost certain the local builder, Paddy Ryan, built all of these houses. He was also responsible for Maryville, another stone house a kilometre away, which he built for Francis Fay. This was later bought and remodelled by the artist Norman Lindsay, and now houses the fascinating Lindsay Museum.

Another interesting stone house was built by Member of Parliament and Mayor of Sydney Town, John Meeks. It was called Everton and can be seen on the highway today.

AUSTRALIAN CAPITAL TERRITORY

Blundell's Farmhouse

DUNTROON STATION,
Australian Capital Territory

c. 1830

Up till 1911 most of the land now contained within the Australian Capital Territory was occupied by nine large sheep stations: Gungahlin, Duntroon, Yarralumla and Uriarra in the north and Tidbinbilla, Tuggeronong, Lanyon, Cuppacumbalong and Booroomba in the south.

Dr Charles Throsby is credited with having discovered the area in 1821, describing it as beautiful undulating grazing country. Settlement began two years later, the district being named Limestone Plains.

The first grant of land on the Plains was obtained by Robert Campbell, a Scottish merchant who, after serving with the family firm in Calcutta, was sent to represent the firm in Sydney Town in 1798. He was instrumental in helping Governor King break the stranglehold the trader-officers of the New South Wales Corps had on the Colony's business. He received his grant in 1821 as partial settlement of a debt of £4000 owed him by the Government and established his property under the name of Pialaga. This was later changed to Duntroon, after the family seat in Argyllshire.

The original Duntroon House was a square cottage with a veranda all round and possibly a detached kitchen and servants' quarters. There is now no sign of the latter, but the main cottage is absorbed into the present building. This is a result of several additions and is now the officers' mess at the Duntroon Military College.

Blundell's Farmhouse was built some distance from the main house for Campbell's chief ploughman, William Ginn, who also enjoyed the right to farm the adjoining 50 acres (20 hectares).

Ginn apparently prospered for he moved in the early 1870s to his own property, making way for George Blundell and his wife Flora (née McLellan).

The Blundells occupied the farmhouse for more than 50 years. During this period their eight children and a number of grandchildren were born there.

The house was originally of four rooms and built of squared rubble stone. The fireplaces and chimneys were of hand-made bricks of a rich colour that combined so well with the warm ochre of the stonework. The roof was covered with shingles.

The windows were six-paned casements with external louvred shutters. The doors were made with three wide boards. The veranda was rubble paved.

The large increase in the Blundell family led to extensions to the back of the house in vertical slab construction and, in 1888, stone additions to the main part of the cottage.

George Blundell was one of a family of 10 children born on Blundell's Hill, less than two kilometres down the river, so he lived out his life within a very small radius.

Blundell's Farmhouse is now being cared for by the Canberra and District Historical Society.

Blundell's Farmhouse

DUNTROON STATION (c. 1830)

Red Beard's Cottage

LANYON,

Australian Capital Territory

1834

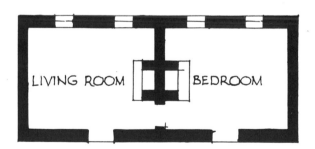

LIVING ROOM   BEDROOM

It was probably sometime before 1828 that the pioneer Timothy Beard settled on a piece of land on the Murrumbidgee River, 30 kilometres south of the centre of Canberra. By January 1834 he had completed a stone dwelling of two rooms on a narrow flat close to the river. With a face distinguished by a flowing red beard it was inevitable that his dwelling should become known as Red Beard's Cottage.

Its construction was simple — rubble walls little more than two metres high with river sand and clay as a mortar. It was smoothed over inside with the same material, had sapling rafters with sawn battens carrying shingles, and stone floors.

There was a large fireplace in each room, back to back on the centre wall. There was another outside fireplace on one of the end walls.

It is uncertain how long Red Beard stayed there but by the end of 1834 there had been some subdivision of land along the river and four 640 acre (256 hectares) blocks had been surveyed. In 1835 John Hamilton Mortimer Lanyon bought one block and James Wright, formerly of Derbyshire, two. Lanyon did not stay for long and by 1836 Wright and his brother William owned all four blocks and had named the property Lanyon.

James Wright acquired more land along the Murrumbidgee, over 4000 acres (1600

hectares), as well as squatting on more at Naas and Booroomba. After marrying, he had slab huts with bark roofs built for himself and his workers and by 1841 there were 59 people living there. These included free immigrants, 25 convicts and six ticket-of-leave men.

A prolonged drought, coupled with a depression in the early 1840s, brought about Wright's bankruptcy, in company with many other landholders of the time.

The run then came into the possession of Andrew Cunningham, a Scottish banker, who went on to acquire considerably more land in what is now the Capital Territory, with Lanyon remaining his headquarters.

The stone kitchen block that still stands near the main homestead, together with a small cottage since demolished, were probably Cunningham's first dwelling. In 1859 the first portion of the now much publicised Lanyon Homestead was built. It has walls of stone, laid as rubble and plastered over, and a shingle roof.

A guest wing of three rooms was added in 1895 and a kitchen wing and bedroom in 1905.

Since being resumed by the Commonwealth Government in 1971, the homestead has been used to house a collection of Sidney Nolan's paintings. These were later moved to a separate gallery and Lanyon is now open to the public as an historic homestead. Red Beard's cottage is now unoccupied but in a reasonable state of preservation.

Red Beard's Cottage

LANYON (1834)

TASMANIA

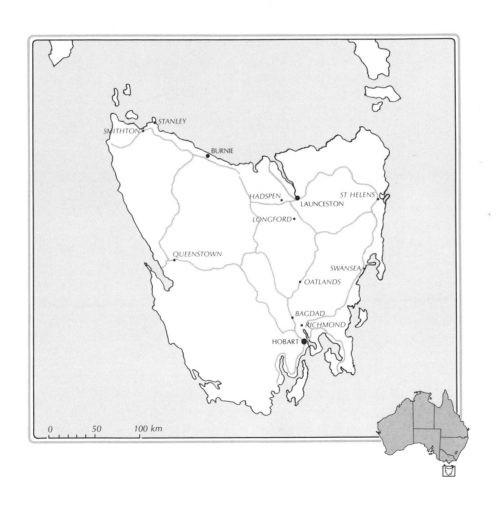

Homestead and Bakehouse

MAYFIELD,

Tasmania

1821

Mayfield Bakehouse

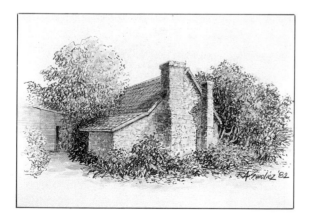

The north and east coasts of Tasmania, or Van Diemen's Land as it was originally called, were reasonably easy of access and provided approaches to good farming land. They were obviously the first to be explored and occupied. The inhospitable west and south were left until later. Even today they remain virtually unoccupied and plans to exploit these areas cause much controversy.

Villages which served farming communities and were home ports for fishing fleets became established relatively early in the island's history. These continue as tourist and fishing centres today, prominent among them St Helens and Swansea.

Not far from Swansea is Mayfield, where one of the earliest grazing properties was set up. Five hundred acres (200 hectares) of land were granted by Governor Sorrell to a Thomas Buxton, an immigrant from Derbyshire, England, who arrived with his family on the *Westmoreland* in 1821.

There is now a large homestead on Mayfield, but the first building was a small stone cottage hastily built during the first year of the Buxton family's occupation.

This cottage consisted of a kitchen and store room and attic room above. The lower floor was below ground level with its ceiling, or the floor for the attic, perhaps half a metre below the eaves line.

By this time the Aborigines had become a serious problem, the blame for which lay mostly with the white invaders. It became necessary for the settlers to take precautions for their own protection. Windows in the cottage were small and, together with the door, were capable of being barred with baulks of timber. The attic was the final retreat. It was reached by a door above the mantlepiece hinged at the bottom so that when opened it hung almost to the floor. After climbing up the door to the room above, it could be hauled up and barred into place. Even if it were noticed it would resist the most determined efforts to prise it open.

One small window at one end of the attic served as a post from which raiders could be observed but was placed too high to provide a means of access.

Bread-baking was an important and necessary function on isolated properties such as this. A feature of Mayfield is a delightfully picturesque bakehouse, pictured, standing close to the first part of the homestead.

A block of six cottages stands on the bank of the Buxton River almost a kilometre from the main dwelling. These were originally provided for the farm workers. Following the English custom they were grouped under the one roof for economy of construction and for warmth during a cold winter. There is a distinctly English look about these dwellings, with attic windows and seven tiny rooms each.

The present owners of Mayfield are Mr and Mrs Dunbabin.

Homestead and Bakehouse

MAYFIELD (1821)

Sayers Court

BAGDAD,

Tasmania

1822

The quaintly named township of Bagdad is on the Midland Highway which connects Hobart with Launceston. The highway follows much the same route as the railway line, although Bagdad itself is a short distance to the west of the railway. It is 37 kilometres from Hobart and 162 kilometres from Launceston.

It is probable that the first white man to see the Bagdad area was the explorer Hugh Germaine, who certainly named it, turning for inspiration to his much-loved *The Arabian Nights*.

The historic property of Sayers Court at Bagdad was purchased by Dr John Espie in 1821. The first part of the homestead was built soon after.

This was a four-square structure of stone with a simple gable roof covered with shingles. It consisted of two main rooms with the inevitable large fireplace.

Twenty-five years later a separate two-storey building was added. It was utilitarian in design but added considerably to the accommodation.

Further additions some time later consisted of a timber wing attached to the rear of the original stone building. A new wing was also added in front of and connecting the original brick buildings.

This later portion is architecturally pleasing with its colonial style and verandas on three sides but is totally at variance with the rest of the Court.

A grim story is told in the area which is a pointer to the attitude of the times. An Aborigine was shot near the property and his body was propped up in a hollow tree. It was held in place with a spear under his chin and allowed to remain there for years, apparently as a warning to the rest of his people.

Sayers Court is still occupied. Miss Dorothy Chalmers lives there under an agreement which ensures her occupancy for the rest of her life.

The third stage of Sayers Court, although well proportioned, is so out of harmony with the two earlier sections as to be quite incongruous. It faces the road and is first to be seen.

Sayers Court

BAGDAD (1822)

Lodge Cottage, Entally House

HADSPEN,

Tasmania

1820s

In 1790 Mary Haydock, a Lancashire lass of 13 years of age, was sentenced to transportation for seven years for horse stealing, thought to be the result of a childish prank. On the ship she met Thomas Reiby, a sub-lieutenant who worked for the East India Company.

Thomas Reiby stayed in Sydney Town and in 1794 married Mary Haydock. They set up a trading establishment, naming it Entally House after a suburb of Calcutta. Reiby died after only 17 years of marriage but Mary, with her two sons, carried on the business. They were very successful, extending it to include, among other things, shipping.

Shipping brought them to Van Diemen's Land (Tasmania) where they bought a warehouse and wharf near Cataract Gorge and 100 acres (40 hectares) of land in the district of Cornwall. They used the name of Entally once again.

The original dwelling on this property appears to have been built in 1820. It was quite small with two square towers with musket slots for defence against bushrangers and Aborigines.

Mary Reiby's two grandsons were educated at Longford Hall Academy in Van Diemen's Land. One of the grandsons, Thomas, went on to Oxford, where he matriculated. He returned to Van Diemen's Land with a wife and took up his inheritance — his father had died while he was away — of 4000 acres (1600 hectares) at Entally, plus another property at Westbury.

Shortly afterwards Thomas Reiby was ordained a Deacon at the Church of Christ, Longford. He was the first Tasmanian to be ordained in his homeland. He was made a priest the following year and his brother James also entered the ministry.

Towards the end of the 1850s Thomas Reiby made extensive additions to the old house. These included more rooms on the ground floor, a second storey and encircling verandas, which, with the stone walls and shingled roofs, give a character and individuality to the building.

The towers were demolished and the stone used to build outhouses and garden walls.

Reiby also had a small stone chapel built, itself a gem, replacing a more primitive building where church services had been held. This followed the English tradition whereby the squire looked after the spiritual needs of his employees.

The lodge cottage, pictured, is also a charming example of a simple stone building with shingle roof and 12-panel colonial windows.

After reaching the eminence of Archdeacon, Thomas Reiby resigned from the Church and later contested and won the seat of Westbury in the Tasmanian House of Assembly. He held the seat for 30 years, serving in several portfolios, including that of Premier from 1876 to 1877.

Entally House is now classified as an Historic Site, administered by the National Parks and Wildlife Service of Tasmania.

Lodge Cottage, Entally House

HADSPEN (1820s)

Christly Church

Christ Church

LONGFORD,
Tasmania

1830s

The district surrounding Longford, a township of 5500 people on the Bass Highway, 27 kilometres from Launceston, was originally known as Norfolk Plains. A number of settlers from Norfolk Island were granted land there in 1813. A Lieutenant Laycock is credited with discovering the area when, six years earlier, he walked from Launceston to Hobart. Known first as Latour, an Irish element in the population caused the name change to Longford.

Christ Church is one of a number of interesting colonial buildings in the town, most of them built by convict labour. Renowned for its stained glass windows and clock, it stands in spacious grounds in which are the graves of many pioneer settlers. Prominent among these are the Dumaresq family.

There were three Dumaresq brothers, all educated at Sandhurst Royal Military College and all migrating to Australia, almost certainly because of a family relationship with Governor Darling. The two elder brothers were given posts with the New South Wales government and later established fairly large land holdings in the Hunter Valley. The youngest of the three, Edward, went to Tasmania. In December 1825 he was put in charge of the Surveyor-General's department.

From 1830 to 1833 he was police magistrate at New Norfolk, after which he settled at Longford and established a grazing property. By the time he died, at the grand old age of 104, he had done much to develop that district.

The entrance gates to the church grounds are dedicated 'to the glory of God and in loving memory of Caroline Dumaresq and her daughter Mary'. Almost overlooked is the unpretentious grave where Tom Roberts is buried. The simple marble plaque records only that he was a 'painter'.

It is difficult to classify the church architecturally for it features elements from a number of periods. The result is unique.

The main structure is built with a predominantly blue local stone which is roughly coursed. A different stone has been used in the tower which is supported above four lancet arched openings. The roof is corrugated galvanised iron painted a rich red. The timber ceilings look pleasantly appropriate.

A modern touch is added by a monument in the grounds carrying a plaque commemorating the 29th World Ploughing Contest sponsored by the National Ploughing Association of Australia. It was held on nearby Mount Ireh Estate on 14-15 June 1982 and was opened by the Rt Hon. Malcolm Fraser, Prime Minister, himself a grazier.

The contest, according to the plaque, brought together ploughmen from Kenya, Osterreich (Austria), Espana (Spain), Canada, Northern Ireland, the United States, Great Britain, Belgie (Belgium), Denmark, Zimbabwe, Deutschland (Germany), Schweiz (Switzerland), Nederland (Holland), Australia, Sverige (Sweden), New Zealand and the Republic of Ireland under the sentiment 'let peace cultivate the fields'.

Christus Church

LONGFORD (1830s)

St Michael's and All Angels Church

BAGDAD,

Tasmania

1830s

Exploration of various parts of the new world attracted adventurous spirits from many parts of eastern Europe and the British Isles. The driving force or motives could be diverse and in many cases were obscure.

There were many strange and adventurous characters. One appears to have been Hugh Germaine, who wandered the Lower Midlands of Van Diemen's Land (Tasmania) during the time of Governor Collins.

Germaine is said to have had two constant companions among his baggage, the Bible and *The Arabian Nights*. That fact itself may not have been remarkable but his habit of going to his books for inspiration when naming geographical features that appealed to him certainly was.

Two townships that are lasting memorials to his idiosyncrasy are Bagdad and Jericho.

Bagdad has many interesting reminders of its past, particularly Sayers Court Homestead and St Michael's and All Angels Church of England.

The Church of England church is a cream-painted timber building, standing in a prominent position. It presents a striking picture with its bright red roof and red-painted bell tower of most original design.

The roof dominates the structure, its trusses countered by flying buttresses of heavy timber along the side walls. The buttresses are on stone footings and bolted back into the wall framing.

Louvred vents add a touch of interest to each side of the gable roof. The bell tower straddles the ridge near the main front and with its metal cross doubling as a lightning arrester, it adds a strong individuality.

The front features an entrance porch with small service rooms on each side and a diamond shaped window in the centre.

St Michael's and All Angels Church

BAGDAD (1830s)

Poets' Cottage

STANLEY,

Tasmania

1830s

Now classified as an Historic Village, Stanley is one of the most interesting centres in Tasmania. It is located on a strange promontory which juts out into Bass Strait almost as far north as the north-western tip of Tasmania. Its outstanding feature is a 150 metre high rocky outcrop now known as The Nut, but named Circular Head by Bass and Flinders in 1798.

The Van Diemen's Land Company was formed in England in 1824 and the following year was granted the north-western tip of Tasmania. By this time most of the land near populated areas had been taken up. The Governor, George Arthur, fearing that such a large company might threaten his authority, directed them to an area that had been investigated several times in the previous two decades and consistently reported as being impenetrable and uninhabitable.

The company spent a large sum of money on developing the area and paid only two small dividends during the next 30-odd years. But the discovery of gold in Tasmania brought boom times to Circular Head and its town of Stanley because of the beef, mutton and potatoes produced there. The produce was supplied to the goldfields and also shipped to the diggings in Victoria.

Dairying, fishing and timber-getting were to follow. The importance of Stanley steadily grew until a new town, Smithton, a short distance away but nearer the fast-growing industries, overtook it.

Stanley has a number of buildings of historic and architectural interest, among them several designed by John Lee Archer, Colonial Architect and for a time a magistrate in Stanley.

Archer's best-known building is the Customs House, but Poets' Cottage, pictured here, shows the same meticulous regard for proportion and a feeling of dignity that characterised all his work.

Poets' Cottage was once a school but was Archer's own home at the time of his death. The name comes from a later occupancy when the cottage was used as a Poets' Collective.

The street front is cement-rendered over stone, with a central entrance door. Two perfectly proportioned 12-paned windows are set symmetrically on each side. The dormer windows to the attic rooms maintain the balance of the whole structure.

Strangely the side and rear walls are in stone, laid as random rubble and the chimneys, of decorative design, are of hand-made bricks.

Poets' Cottage

STANLEY (1830s)

Miller's Cottage and Mill

OATLANDS,

Tasmania

1830s

The Mill Complex

One of the oldest groups of buildings in Oatlands, Tasmania, is the Callington Mill complex, currently being restored by the National Parks and Wildlife Service. Oatlands' first building was a courthouse built in 1829. The first part of the mill was erected in 1830.

Governor Macquarie made a tour of inspection of Van Diemen's Land (Tasmania) in 1811, passing through Oatlands during this tour. But it was not until his second visit, 10 years later, that he named the site, declaring it 'a very eligible station for a town'.

The then Governor, Lieutenant-Colonel George Arthur, was fortunate in having the services of skilled stonemasons and carpenters in the building of the town. Many of them were from the disbanded Royal Staff Corps who had earlier been stationed in the area to guard the farmers and tradesmen from Aborigines.

John Jubilee Vincent first operated the mill, commencing in October 1837, and in July 1840 it was reported as producing 30 bushels of flour per hour. It was fitted with steam and wind power to drive two pairs of grinding stones. In 1880 it was modernised with a 14 horse-power engine and began producing about six tons daily.

The complex consisted of an owner's dwelling of 12 rooms, two smaller cottages, stables and coach house, miller's cottage, grain and flour stores, cow shed and piggeries. The mill ceased to operate towards the end of last century.

The miller's cottage measures five metres by three metres and consists of two rooms and an attic. The larger room has a fireplace at one end and steep stairs, little more than a ladder providing access to the attic.

Little thought was given to the miller's comfort in the planning, for the only access to the tiny bedroom is from the outside. It must have been an ordeal to leave the comfort of a log fire and walk out into a freezing Tasmanian winter to reach the bedroom. Possibly the attic was the preferred sleeping quarters and the bedroom used mainly as an office.

The thick stone walls are laid in coursed rubble with some quite large stones used, especially at the corners. Sills are the usual single stone and lintels at window and door heads are quite massive, testifying to the skill of the masons. The stone walls are comparatively high as the rafters spring from a point some 400 millimetres above the attic floor. The roof is covered with split shingles.

Miller's Cottage and Mill

OATLANDS (1830s)

St John's Church

RICHMOND,

Tasmania

1837

Richmond is probably the only town in Australia where you can become completely lost in the past. Its streets of charming colonial architecture have an authentic atmosphere of more than 150 years ago. It can boast among other things the oldest bridge and the oldest Roman Catholic church in Australia. St Luke's Church of England was built two years earlier in 1834.

Lieutenant John Bowen led a party which explored Richmond in 1803 and discovered coal, thus accounting for the name Coal River.

An Irishman named John Cassidy was one of the earliest settlers, arriving with his family in 1810 and naming his property Woodburn.

In 1835 the first Catholic bishop to be appointed to Australia, Dr Polding, visited Hobart Town on his way to Port Jackson. Until that time Australia had been under the ecclesiastical jurisdiction of the Bishop of Mauritius.

Bishop Polding celebrated mass in John Cassidy's house. Stirred by the bishop's visit, the Catholic community discussed the need for a church. Cassidy gave the land and within weeks £700 had been raised which was augmented by a grant of £500 from the Governor.

St John's was not designed especially for Richmond. It was built to plans for an English country church brought out by Bishop Polding.

It was opened on the last day of 1837.

It was originally a simple rectangular building in what can best be described as a modified early Gothic style. The ashlar stonework that was to become a hallmark of the period was used.

The church assumed a more Gothic character with additions in 1859. These consisted of the sacristy, chancel and a rather overpowering porch, tower and spire.

Within the tower is a stone, spiral staircase leading to the choir gallery.

The original tower was very tall. In 1893 it was replaced by a much shorter version with more detailed work around its base. Even this was demolished in 1972. The copper-sheathed spire which now rises above the tower is a compromise in height between the two earlier ones and is much simpler in design.

Reading between the lines in the old marriage register one learns that the community was mostly engaged in lowly occupations, many were convicts, some recently freed. The record of church collections is also revealing. The collection for Sunday, 14 November 1841 was 1/1½d and for 5 June 1842, 1/2d.

And inscriptions on the headstones tell graphic stories of the violent times of early Richmond and of all Van Diemen's Land (Tasmania).

St John's Church

RICHMOND (1837)

Lyons' Cottage

STANLEY,

Tasmania

1840s

Stanley, on Circular Head (The Nut), Tasmania, is so steeped in the early history of the Colony that it has been proclaimed an Historic Village by the Tasmanian branch of the National Trust of Australia. Many of the original buildings have been preserved near the wharf that once saw old whalers, sailing ships and cargo vessels loading produce for various destinations, most notably the Victorian goldfields.

Other buildings and dwellings designed in the colonial version of the Georgian style, then popular in England, can be seen further around at the base of The Nut (the present-day name for Circular Head) and along the road around Tatlows Beach.

Stanley can also claim to have been the birthplace of the only Tasmanian-born Prime Minister of Australia, Joseph Aloysius Lyons. The little cottage that was his birthplace and another where he spent much of his childhood are now presented as tourist attractions.

Born in 1879, Joseph Lyons was one of a large family. His father was not robust and experienced difficulty in providing for his family. Joseph began work early in life, obtaining his first job at the age of five! By the time he was twelve he had been errand boy in a general store, messenger in a newspaper office, scrub-cutter and farm labourer.

His early years were spent mostly with two aunts in the house pictured. It was not far from his birthplace and in the vicinity of Poets' Cottage.

It is unpretentious, as are most of the earlier houses in Stanley, but in its very simplicity suggests a feeling for design not always found in more ambitious dwellings. The Georgian influence is apparent in the symmetrical placing of the 12-paned windows and the central door. Its cream-painted weatherboard walls reflect in certain lights the surrounding green of the Tasmanian countryside.

At the age of 19 Joseph Lyons qualified as a teacher in the Tasmanian Education Department. In 1909 he stood as Labor candidate for the seat of Wilmot in the Tasmanian House of Assembly and was elected. He became Premier and Minister for Railways in 1923.

In 1929 he was elected member for Wilmot in the Federal Parliament. Disillusioned by the intrigue within the party he switched to the conservatives in 1931 and formed the United Australia Party.

The new party was returned to power in December of the same year and Joseph Aloysius Lyons became Prime Minister and Treasurer. He was married in 1915 and died in 1939 survived by his wife, Dame Enid Lyons, also a noted Member of Parliament, five sons and six daughters.

Lyons' Cottage

STANLEY (1840s)

QUEENSLAND

ROCKHAMPTON

MARYBOROUGH

ROMA

KINGAROY
CHINCHILLA

DALBY

PETRIE

TOOWOOMBA
DRAYTON   IPSWICH   BRISBANE

WARWICK

GOONDIWINDI

0   100 km   N S W

Typical Queensland Outback Dwelling

In every country of the world there has developed what has become known as a typical dwelling. Australia is no exception.

After the split slab and bark huts of the early pioneers a more sophisticated character appeared in the dwellings. The colony had developed sufficiently to have joinery such as doors and windows available and imported materials in sufficient quantity. The material that played the most important part in the change was corrugated galvanised iron. Relatively easy to transport, even over the rough tracks of the day, it showed up in the most unlikely places and was used almost indiscriminately on roofs and walls. The veranda, which had become almost universal in Australian dwellings, was covered with bull-nosed iron, so named for its rounded shape.

This house, north of Goondiwindi in Queensland, is typical of thousands in the tropical and semi-tropical parts of the continent. In the far north it was often elevated on timber piers or stumps to allow a current of air to pass under the house for cooling it and also as some protection from termites.

Generally, the construction of the typical house was orthodox — a plate and stud frame with high ceilings as it was thought that this contributed to a cool interior. The walls, especially where there was a veranda, were lined only on the inside, the framework of studs showing on the outside.

In many cases the wall bracing was placed between adjacent studs in the form of a diagonal cross. This was usually set out, either deliberately or by chance, to form an interesting pattern.

Doors were often quite narrow, usually in pairs as shutters known as French windows. Veranda posts were surmounted by brackets, often quite ornamental in design. Their purpose was to reduce the span of the plates and minimise the possibility of sagging.

Bathrooms were rare, but when they were included they were usually under the veranda roof, usually at one of the rear corners adjacent to the water tank.

Time and neglect have not dealt kindly with this further example of a typical country dwelling. The custom of omitting outside linings to walls under verandas where weatherproofing is not important can be seen.

Typical Queensland Outback Dwelling

Mostowie

PETRIE,

Queensland

1840s

The Bell family figured prominently in the development of Queensland. Their saga began with an Irish immigrant, Thomas Bell, and his three sons who between them acquired several grazing properties. They alternatively flourished and languished along with the fortunes of the Colony, which were largely determined by periods of prosperity interspersed with recessions and droughts.

Mostowie, near Petrie, was not one of the early Bell properties. It was part of a large area of land selected in the 1840s by a man called Joyner who grazed it for a period before it was cut up into a number of smaller blocks. That on which Mostowie stood, 180 acres (72 hectares) was a dairy farm. It was purchased by Mrs Mary Bell and her daughter Cecil in 1951. The age of the building was then recognised as over 100 years, although some remodelling had taken place.

Though not a planning masterpiece, the layout of the house originally was typical of the day, by which time the needs of an almost tropical climate were recognised. There was a veranda all round, and a hall straight through the centre with rooms opening off it on each side. By opening the doors at each end of the hall a movement of cool air was achieved on the hottest day. There was also a large attic room.

The kitchen with one other room were in a separate block connected to the main house by a walkway.

Built of cedar and beech and standing on a knoll which commanded a magnificent view, it had a charm and a character all its own. It has now disappeared under the waters of the Petrie Dam, built in the 1970s.

Figuring largely in Mostowie's history is its ghost.

Miss Cecil Bell has said: 'I used to sleep in the attic, and I had a Great Dane dog whom I used to tie up at the top of the stairs. On a few occasions I woke in the night with a peculiar feeling of someone coming in from the original narrow attic ladder — like steps — and my Great Dane — who was *not* afraid — standing with his hackles up and growling and snarling and looking at the entrance to the steps. It was eerie. But as I did not panic, shriek or yell the ghost became very friendly. This is a fact.'

Mostowie

PETRIE (1840s)

Boat Builder's Dwelling

BRISBANE RIVER,

Queensland

1855

The area around the Brisbane River was first explored by Lieutenant John Oxley in 1823 while seeking a site for a penal settlement. He recommended Redcliff Point. In September 1824 Oxley, together with Robert Hoddle, a Lieutenant Millar of the 40th Regiment and a detachment of troops, established a depot at Humpybong.

Hoddle had recently completed a survey of Bell's Line of Road, which extended from Windsor through Kurrajong Heights to Lithgow and provided an alternative route over the Blue Mountains in New South Wales.

When Oxley later changed his recommendation for a town site to what is now North Quay, the new site was confirmed by the Chief Justice. It was called Edinglassie, a name derived from a combination of the Scottish Edinborough and Glasgow.

This name was later changed to Brisbane Town but the change was not recognised until 1839. In the intervening period several unsuccessful attempts had been made to relocate the town at Stradbroke Island and Cleveland.

Prisoners sent to the new penal settlement were 'colonially convicted' — a term used to describe those originally transported from Great Britain who had committed fresh crimes in New South Wales.

While Brisbane remained a penal settlement the opening of land to free settlement was delayed. It was not until the early 1840s when the last of the prisoners had departed and the gaols closed that free settlers began to develop land along Brisbane River and Moreton Bay.

The Colony of Queensland was proclaimed on 6 June 1859. Until this time it was part of New South Wales.

This picture is a reconstruction of part of the settlement along the banks of the Brisbane River in 1855. In the foreground, on the approximate site of the Victoria Bridge today, is a boat builder's house, typical of the riverside dwellings of the day.

Walls were of vertical slabs, shaped to fit into channels cut in the top and bottom plates of round, roughly dressed logs. The spaces between were packed with river mud mixed with grass.

The roof was covered with shingles.

The early settlers were fortunate in having the choice of several good building timbers, one of the best being hoop pine. This fine timber was once plentiful in southern Queensland and the north coast of New South Wales but is now almost cut out.

Immediately behind the boat builder's house was a timber storage shed. Its walls were slotted for drying boat building timber. Close at hand was the chimney from the furnace which supplied the heat for the steaming process.

Cradles in which the hulls of boats were shaped were a common sight along the river bank, while across the waterway could be seen the clustering dwellings of the growing town.

Log fences marked out the often oddly shaped blocks of land on which the riverside homes were built. Logs were driven into the ground fairly close together and a horizontal log wired near the top to afford a degree of stability.

Boat Builder's Dwelling

BRISBANE RIVER (1855)

Chinchilla Station

DARLING DOWNS,

Queensland

1850s

The story of the discovery and settlement of Queensland's Darling Downs is one of courage, frustration and finally triumph. The credit for the discovery by a white man goes to Alan Cunningham.

When still part of the colony of New South Wales the route from Sydney to Moreton Bay was via the coast. It was in 1828 that Cunningham, looking for an alternative route, crossed the Great Dividing Range at a point now known as Cunningham's Gap. He reached what he described as a 'well watered valley, affording abundance of the richest pasturage'.

Despite his strenuous efforts to interest others in the newly found Downs, it was not until 1840 that the first settler, Patrick Leslie, accompanied by one assigned convict, came north and selected a site on the Condamine River.

He was joined a month later by his brother Walter who, with 21 ticket-of-leave men, had overlanded 5700 sheep. Thus Canning Downs Station, the first on the Darling Downs, was established.

The brothers built a slab hut with a bark roof, later building a larger house with the original hut serving as a detached kitchen. The city of Warwick now covers part of the original Canning Downs Station.

Sheep played an important part in the development of the western and northern sections of the Downs. When Captain Phillip Gidley King arranged for 26 Spanish merino sheep to be brought from South Africa, the 13 survivors of the rigorous journey were sold to a number of landholders. Some of their progeny found their way north.

Chinchilla Station was selected soon after Canning Downs. The split slab house, pictured, was built on it in the mid-80s. It may have been occupied at first by the station owners, but it is known that Mr and Mrs James Riden lived there from 1888 to 1899. Mrs Riden was born on the station in 1863, the daughter of a station hand named Peter McGregor.

The walls are of split slabs fitting into adzed plates, top and bottom, and lined with newspapers. Windows are hinged wooden shutters.

Rafters are saplings, originally covered with bark then shingles and now corrugated galvanised iron. The house is divided into four rooms, the internal walls again being split slabs.

There is a veranda in front, probably an addition, as was often the case. Its roof is supported by adzed plates carried on square posts.

The frame of this house is ironbark and cypress pine while the slabs are of a comparatively rare timber known by the Aborigines as 'budgeroo'. Its botanical name is *Lyscarpus ternifolia*.

Chinchilla Station

DARLING DOWNS (1850s)

St Anne's Church of England Church

JONDARYAN,
Queensland

1859

St Anne's at Jondaryan was the second Anglican church built on the Darling Downs.

Jondaryan Station was established on land taken up in 1842 by Charles Coxon. By 1859 it had passed into the hands of three brothers, Robert, Edward and Frederick Tooth. The church was built on their property.

The first service was held in October 1859 not long after that at St Matthews at Drayton. The area was still within the diocese of Newcastle.

Like most of the early dwellings, the Jondaryan church was built on relatively low ground to be near a source of water. Life on the Downs was rudely interrupted in 1893 by a massive flood. The floor of the church remained just above water level, giving refuge to the Tooth brothers and their station hands.

Later that year, however, the building was moved and re-erected with minor alterations on its present hillside site. It was open then to all denominations, possibly because other churches had suffered in the flood.

The main structural material is thought to be offcuts from timber being prepared for railway sleepers, sawn flat on one face, rounded on the other. The spaces between the vertical wall slabs are covered with narrow battens after the style of lap and space construction. The roof is supported by king post trusses. The roof framing and walls are timber lined.

Not far from Jondaryan, at Aubigny, is the Lutheran church of St John's.

A group of German migrants, fleeing from religious persecution in their homeland, arrived in Sydney in the early 1850s. Their Consul directed them to the Downs where an acute shortage of manpower had developed, following the discovery of gold in the northern fields.

From a small beginning their number had grown to 11,000 within 10 years, most receiving grants of land from a grateful government. A place of worship figured high on their priorities so St John's was built.

It, too, is built of sawn timbers on an orthodox frame and stands on stumps which lift it half a metre or more above the ground. Unique features of St John's, however, are the triangular buttresses which also stand on stumps.

A water tank at the rear of the church, equipped with an enamel mug, speaks of compassion for the casual passer-by. But a reflection on the present-day traveller is the need for a chain which secures the mug to the tank. Adjoining the church is a burial ground with headstones giving a potted history of the Lutheran community.

St Anne's Church of England Church

JONDARYAN (1859)

Log Cabin

GLENMORE STATION,

Queensland

1859

The Fitzroy River, some 600 kilometres north of Brisbane, was discovered in 1853 by Charles and William Archer. They named the river after the New South Wales Governor of the day.

At the time the Archers were pastoralists with a property at Wallerawang near Lithgow. They decided to transfer to the much richer country of the Darling Downs and set off with several thousand sheep.

The animals contracted a disease on the way which meant long rest stops. By the time they reached the Downs all of what they considered suitable land had been taken up. They pushed on to the Fitzroy River but it was to be two years after they had started out that their epic journey ended.

The New South Wales Crown Lands Commissioner, who was later sent to find a site for a township on the river, wanted to name it Charleston after Charles Archer. Archer declined the honour and the town was named Rockhampton, after a group of rocks in the river and the English birthplace (Hampton) of the Commissioner, William Henry Wiseman.

The Archers settled on the banks of a lagoon and called their property Gracemere.

Shortly afterwards a second grazing property was established by a Mr S. B. Birkbeck nearby and named Glenmore. Birkbeck imported a number of Mexican tradesmen in 1860 to build a large adobe homestead.

The first dwelling on the property, however, was the log cabin, pictured, thought to have been built by a Canadian in 1859. Two years later a nearby hotel, of mainly vertical slab construction, was acquired and moved to Glenmore. Finally a Mexican mason added a stone house of several rooms to the collection of unique buildings.

The log cabin is built in the traditional Canadian way, introduced into Canada by northern European migrants. Full logs are used, notched and interlocked at the corners and piled one on top of the other. It results in a very substantial structure.

There is a window opening at each end of the cabin, formed by cutting out a piece from two adjoining logs. Sufficient timber is left at the top of one and the bottom of the other to avoid weakening the wall.

The roof is framed up with sapling rafters and was originally covered with long split boards lapped so that they resembled continuous shingles. The gable ends were filled in with similar split boards.

Walls are lined internally with bark in large sheets fixed vertically. The gable ends do not appear to have been lined and as there was no ceiling, natural shrinkage soon added to the ventilation.

The cabin is still in use, mainly as a store room.

As a sequel to the Archer story it is interesting to note that the area soon proved unsuitable for sheep and the graziers turned to cattle. Further, the town of Rockhampton has owed its phenomenal growth first to gold and copper from Mount Morgan, 30 kilometres away, and more recently coal.

Log Cabin

GLENMORE STATION (1859)

St Matthew's Church of England Church

DRAYTON,

Queensland

1887

The first Anglican Church on the Darling Downs of Queensland was built at Drayton in 1859. Prior to that Canon Glennie held services in the Bull's Head Inn and later in the court house from about 1848. Queensland was then part of New South Wales and Drayton was included in the diocese of Newcastle. (Drayton was first called The Springs and where Toowoomba now stands was The Swamp.)

Benjamin Glennie was born in England, one of twelve children of a school master. As a young man he travelled extensively in Europe as a tutor to the children of wealthy families who were doing the fashionable Grand Tour. He acquired a fluency in a number of languages after his travels.

Two months after landing in Australia, in 1848, he was ordained a deacon at Morpeth. Soon afterwards he was sent to the Moreton Bay Parish, which included most of what is now Queensland. He appears to have developed a special interest in the Darling Downs.

At an auction sale in the Drayton court house in 1850 Canon Glennie bought two blocks of land in the newly surveyed township for £15. A kitchen was built on this land and Canon Glennie moved in. A year later a slab parsonage was completed, as well as a hut for the Canon's servants.

The parsonage consisted of three rooms, with a movable partition between the middle and west rooms. This was taken out on Sundays to convert the parsonage into a place of worship.

The year the first church was built (1859) — on another site — Queensland became a sovereign Colony and the Darling Downs part of the diocese of Brisbane. Canon Glennie walked to Brisbane for the enthronement of the new Bishop. He later acquired a horse but more often than not he walked, leading the animal. This was probably partly out of sympathy for his four-legged companion and partly because of his poor horsemanship.

In 1887 a church was built opposite the parsonage. Now a stone cairn on the corner of Cambooya and Rudd Streets marks the site.

The church was built of split slabs, fixed vertically, with top and bottom plates. A small bell tower perched somewhat incongruously on the main gable end of the shingle-covered roof.

When this church was deemed too small for the growing centre of Drayton a piece of land was acquired in a commanding situation on the hill overlooking the township. Four years later the foundation stone for the present St Matthew's was laid.

When more land adjoining the new church was acquired the church, pictured here, was moved from Cambooya and Rudd Streets to serve as a Sunday School.

The main building material of the new St Matthew's was a local bluestone, a very hard volcanic lava. It is laid as ashlar, the face being vermiculated, with tooled margins. The porch and dressings are sandstone.

The interior is distinguished by hammer beam roof trusses and white-painted rendered walls. A three-light lancet headed window is a prominent feature at the eastern end.

St Matthew's Church of England Church

DRAYTON (1887)

WESTERN AUSTRALIA

KALGOORLIE

PERTH

FREMANTLE

NORSEMAN

BUNBURY

COCANARUP

KATANNING

JERRAMUNGUP

ESPERANCE

MOUNT BARKER

ALBANY

0   150 km

Jerramungup Homestead

JERRAMUNGUP,

Western Australia

1850

A number of sea captains and sailors figured among Australia's early settlers. One such was a Captain Hassell who was lured to the west by the charm of a beautiful natural harbour, a coastline of rocky cliffs with clean sandy beaches at intervals and a backcloth of dense karri forests. He saw the possibilities and forsook the sea for a life in the new land.

He applied for and was granted 20,000 acres (8000 hectares) along the bank of the Gardiner River not far from Albany. It was a disappointing position as the river water was salty and of no use for stock. Rainwater was the only source of supply for both the animals and the household.

In 1850 Captain Hassell began to build a hut.

As distinct from so many of the early settlers the Hassells, Mrs Hassell in particular, befriended the natives and as a consequence received much help from them. The name for their property, Jerramungup, is an Aboriginal word which translates roughly into 'land of tall trees, rocks and water'.

The original Hassell house, pictured here, was truly a product of the land. The walls are of stone, roughly squared but laid as rubble, the timber jarrah and the roof thatched with a combination of river grass and scrub timber.

The stone of the walls was laid in river mud as mortar and the walls were up to 750 millimetres thick. Heavy beams of jarrah spanned window and door openings. Doors were low and narrow, 1800 millimetres high by 600 millimetres wide, with windows a little wider. The imported sashes had the small panes that were the fashion at the time.

A veranda afforded some shade to the front of the house, its covering merely a continuation of the main roof with a slight bell-cast. It was supported on round poles for posts and plate.

Inside, the building was divided into two rooms, one further partitioned off by means of a curtain. The main room was the kitchen and it still contains the enormous old fireplace and the bread-baking oven.

The fireplace takes up almost the full length of the wall and is set out from the wall, a necessary provision to ensure that the chimney remained well away from the thatch of the roof.

The timbers used for the roof construction were mainly mulga trees and, as there is no ceiling, they can be clearly seen.

In 1906, a new house of stone and brick was built and lived in by the Hassell family for six years. Reduced now to 1400 hectares, Jerramungup is now owned by Mrs L. Parsons.

Jerramungup Homestead

JERRAMUNGUP (1850)

Dempster House

ESPERANCE,

Western Australia

1860s

The first recorded entry of ships into Esperance Bay in Western Australia was in 1792 when two French frigates took refuge from a gale. One was called *L'Esperance*, which translates as 'expectation'. This appropriate name was given to the bay.

Matthew Flinders was there in 1820 and John Eyre in 1841, but it was not until 1863 that real settlement began, and that was overland from Northam. The journey was undertaken by Andrew and C. E. Dempster.

They were encouraged to settle at Esperance by regulations which came into force early in 1864, making land rent free for the first four years if it were taken up for a period of 12 years. The Dempster brothers obtained 340,000 acres (136,616 hectares). They brought with them 518 sheep, 80 head of cattle and 19 horses on the 550 kilometre trek from Northam.

A wattle and daub shelter was quickly built but this soon gave way to the imposing homestead which stands in what is now Dempster Street.

Built principally of stone, the main part has the appearance of semi-detached cottages. It is roofed as two distinct entities with a box gutter through the centre. The parapet on the main front which almost hides the front section of the roof is most unusual for that time.

The stonework at the sides extends beyond the roof line, finishing as raking parapets. Walls more than six metres high give the ceiling the impression of being almost beyond reach.

A chapel is incorporated within the main part of the building, reminiscent of the English custom when there were a number of employees on an estate.

The veranda along the main front breaks up the severity of the building. Long wings at the rear extend some distance from the main part of the building, the lower walls and simpler style suggesting lesser importance.

Andrew Dempster married and was blessed by a large family. Later he moved to Muresk, where he established another farm, now the Muresk Agriculture College.

The success of the Dempsters' farming venture attracted other settlers to the Esperance district. It was not long before the Moir brothers established themselves at Fanny Cove. Derelict remains of other early stone homesteads are to be seen along the Thomas River.

The town of Esperance grew in importance after the discovery of gold at Coolgardie, when it became the main port for the goldfields. This importance was relatively short-lived as the opening of the Perth to Coolgardie railway dealt it a severe blow. However, it has now regained much of its former stature as new soil technology and improved farming methods have uncovered a much greater value in the surrounding farming properties.

The house is now owned and occupied by the Hon. D. Wordsworth, Member of the Legislative Council of Western Australia, and has been faithfully restored and furnished in period style.

RA Smolicz '82

Dempster House

ESPERANCE (1860s)

Cull House

ALBANY,

Western Australia

1870s

UPPER FLOOR

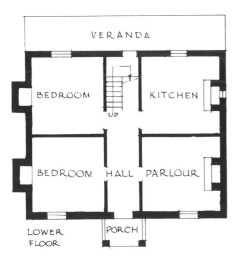

LOWER FLOOR

There stands a house at 250 Middleton Road, Albany, which, while no architectural gem, has a fascinating history. More than 110 years old, the saga of its building is a tale of dogged determination and untiring effort.

When an Irishman, Matthew Cull, and his Welsh-born wife Sarah Ann (née Bagg), migrated to Australia he found work on the wharves at Albany. In 1870 he obtained a small two acre (0.8 hectare) piece of land over the observatory hill and about three kilometres from the wharves. There he erected a temporary dwelling of bark.

It was surrounded by thick scrub, penetrated only by a maze of Aboriginal tracks, but there was a fresh water stream a short distance up the hill.

Each morning on his way to work Matthew Cull pushed a wheel barrow up the track to the crest of the hill, where he loaded it with rocks and left it there for the day. In the evening he wheeled the loaded barrow down again to his temporary dwelling.

Frequently in winter he made the homeward trek after dark which was quite difficult in the heavy scrub. There were times when he missed the way and wandered off on one of the many cross tracks. When he did not arrive home at his usual time his wife sensed what had happened. She would then stand outside the bark hut and with shrill coo-ees guide her bushed husband home.

Eventually Matthew accumulated sufficient stone to build the footings for the ambitious house he planned. It was to be of two storeys, with four rooms and central hall on each floor.

The next task was to make the bricks. As all walls, both exterior and within the building are of brick, this in itself was no mean effort. It is not recorded how long it took.

Using the minimum of tools, the house is a monument to its builder's ingenuity. Lacking a spirit level, he used a long medicine bottle filled with water as a level and this, with his home-made plumb bob, helped him achieve a remarkable degree of accuracy.

The heavy timbers in the house are karri, a local wood of great strength. There is a continuous 300 millimetre deep beam extending right across the building, affording support to the stair and the rear wall of the upper floor.

The roof covering is imported corrugated galvanised iron, still the original and in good order despite its proximity to the sea.

Each room has a fireplace, those on the eastern side being within the outer wall, those on the west projecting beyond it. The reason for this variation is now not known.

When their house was completed, Matthew and Sarah Ann devoted themselves assiduously to other pursuits. They raised a family of 15 children and after diverting the water from the nearby stream to the property developed an extensive vegetable garden. They found a ready market for their produce in the fast-growing town of Albany.

The present occupant of the house is a grandson, Mr Ron Cull. He was born there and has lived there all his life except for a period spent in New Guinea during World War II.

Cull House

ALBANY (1870s)

St Werburgh's Chapel

MOUNT BARKER,
Western Australia

1873

Roof trusses are secured in a novel way. A vertical member is carried down the face of the wall and bolted through it. The upper bolt also holds a plate for the veranda rafters, while the lower bolt has a metal plate on the outer face.

The story of St Werburgh's Chapel really begins a lot earlier than its building in 1873. It could be said to begin in the year 1836 when a young lieutenant of the 51st Regiment, George Egerton-Warburton, arrived at Albany on his way to Van Diemen's Land (later Tasmania) in charge of a shipload of convicts.

The youngest son of Piet Egerton-Warburton of Arley, Cheshire, England, he apparently carried an introduction to the Colony's former Government Resident, Sir Richard Spencer, for during the break in his journey at Albany he stayed with the Resident's family at Strawberry Hill (see page 110).

Lieutenant Egerton-Warburton completed the voyage to Van Diemen's Land but when a short time later he was ordered to India, he sold his commission and returned to Albany. In 1842 he and Augusta Spencer were married and settled at the Strawberry Hill Farm in Albany for a short period before moving on to St Werburgh's, Mount Barker.

When Augusta Egerton-Warburton died in 1871, her husband's brother, in his dual capacity as Squire of Arley and Rector of the local church, sent the sum of £500 to build a chapel at St Werburgh's. The Egerton-Warburtons decided to build the chapel themselves and endow it with the Squire of Arley's gift.

The name of the chapel's designer is not on record but the building is certainly unique. The construction was undertaken by George Egerton-Warburton and some of his eight sons, assisted by one Meshack Parsons, an employee.

The walls were made of local clay, pugged and rammed into frames in a continuous monolithic form. When the clay had dried and set the frames were removed, wall surfaces dressed with an adze, and door and window openings cut out with a crosscut saw.

An Albany carpenter, Mr Blechynden, who appears to have given his services free, was responsible for the woodwork, framing up the roof and covering it with sheoak shingles. The shingles have since been replaced with corrugated galvanised iron. Sheoak and jarrah timbers were used for the joinery.

The timber-lined ceiling is coved, ceiling joists occurring a metre or so up the rafters. Tie beams at plate level prevent any tendency of roof or walls to spread.

Decorative hand-made wrought iron was also the work of the Egerton-Warburtons.

The encircling veranda, rather like a colonnade, not only gives shade and shelter in a climate that can be extreme at times, but also provides protection from the elements for the clay pug walls.

A unique feature of the furnishings is the font, which had been the family mortar for many years. It had been used to grind grain for the wholemeal flour which was perhaps the staple diet of the period.

A memorial to George Edward Egerton-Warburton in the grounds puts the date of erection as 1873. The chapel was consecrated in 1874.

In 1978 a cyclone destroyed the bell tower and caused other structural damage to the building. Restoration was completed three years later.

St Werburgh's Chapel

MOUNT BARKER (1873)

Cocanarup Homestead

COCANARUP,

Western Australia

1876

The story of Cocanarup Station is one of hardship, disappointment and remarkable achievement that typified the indomitable pioneering spirit of the early settlers.

The site for the station was chosen by a John Dunn in 1868. A good supply of water was assured by a permanent spring which gave the property its name, Cocanarup, which was an Aboriginal word for 'place where water ends'. John Dunn took up a lease of 28,603 acres (11,500 hectares).

In three years Dunn had cleared sufficient land for him to bring the first sheep into the district. This meant an arduous journey from Albany with the animals in drays and bullock waggons. He was helped by his brother, George, and another settler named John Moir.

The route that John Dunn later took in transporting his wool by dray to Jerramungup is essentially that followed by the present main road to Albany. In 1873 George Dunn took the wool over the same route. He did not return but his place was taken by three other brothers.

The normal hazards of pioneer life were added to by marauding Aborigines who were stealing sheep and robbing camps. John Moir suffered the same troubles. In 1876 he captured two of the natives and locked them up, intending to hand them over to the police at Esperance. But when he took them a meal they grabbed a knife and stabbed him to death.

Four years later John Dunn was waylaid and stabbed.

The present homestead and a blacksmith's shop were completed in 1876. They were constructed essentially of stone laid as random rubble, set in a mortar made of sandy soil and locally burnt lime. A shearing shed and stable were later built by a convict stonemason who had escaped from South Australia and walked around the coast.

The buildings were roofed with the corrugated galvanised iron that was then imported from England and that was to play a large part in the early buildings in Western Australia. The veranda, its roof supported on sawn posts and plates, was probably a later addition.

James Dunn's discovery of payable gold, about six kilometres from the homestead, in 1898 brought about a great change in life at Cocanarup. Interest in the grazing property quickly waned as gold and copper took over and for a while the quiet and lonely countryside was invaded by fortune hunters.

The Dunn connection with Cocanarup appears to have lasted until 1907. There were at least three other owners in the years up to 1923 when the property was abandoned.

During the Depression years charcoal burning was carried on in the area. The charcoal was burnt in pits and some of the iron was removed from the roofs of Cocanarup and used to cover the pits.

In 1944 the homestead was bought for £75 by a retired postmaster from Ravensthorpe and it has remained with his family. It has now been restored and is occupied by Gordon and Coralie Thomas.

Cocanarup Homestead

COCANARUP (1876)

Early Shops and Dwellings

NORSEMAN,

Western Australia

1890s

Norseman, midway between Kalgoorlie and Esperance, is on the fringe of the great gold-mining area of Western Australia, but it is rich in such a variety of minerals that large scale prospecting is still being carried on.

Gold was first discovered there in 1894. The rush that followed reached its peak in 1901 after the fabulous Royal Reef was discovered. The population rose to 1593. Norseman is still the location of the richest operating gold mine in Australia.

Western Australia was well into its galvanised iron era when the township began to grow. It became the major material for the first hastily erected buildings and still remained much in evidence in the more substantial structures that eventually followed. Iron was always the first choice for roofing in such a low rainfall area.

The adjoining attached buildings, pictured, were typical of the shop and dwelling type structures of the late nineteenth century. Following the European tradition they were built with cellars for storage and with a dwelling behind the shop premises.

The corrugated galvanised iron clad walls were built without windows. Light entered the rooms through skylights. The walls were lined inside as well as out with the corrugated material. The wells of the skylights, which were shaped as truncated pyramids to spread the light, featured flat galvanised iron.

Display windows were glazed with the largest panes then available with wooden glazing bars of quite stout construction. A veranda, supported on dressed wooden posts, gave windows and goods protection from the sun and projected out to the gutter of the then tree-lined roadway.

Ceilings were lined with hessian and later with lath and plaster.

The general store, which was operated by the present owner, Mrs Ada Elizabeth Lea, for 48 years, is now a bookshop. The second shop and dwelling was the banking chamber for the Bank of New South Wales, carrying the familiar 'Established 1817' on the parapet, and behind it the residence for the manager.

Norseman's population now remains steady at 3000 and the township is complete with all the modern facilities needed to serve such a community.

Early Shops and Dwellings

NORSEMAN (1890s)

Old Strawberry Hill Farm

ALBANY,
Western Australia

1836

The task of deciding on the location for the first settlement in the west of the continent was given to a Major Lockyer. He decided on Albany at King George's Sound in 1826 and it was not until 1900 that the change was made to Fremantle as the port of call for overseas vessels.

Although Albany has now declined it was, by the turn of the century, well established as a flourishing and attractive town.

Reports from Lockyer's successor, Captain Wakefield, in 1827, refer to a garden and maize crop at a farm about two miles east of the town. He also noted two huts which housed stockmen in charge of cattle and sheep. The next year Lieutenant George Sleeman is reported to have cut a road to the farm and planted three acres of vegetables.

When the centre of government was moved from Albany to Perth in 1832 the farm was leased and although a few hectares of wheat was grown little development is recorded. But when Sir Richard Spencer was appointed Government Resident at Albany soon afterwards a new era began.

Sir Richard bought the farm, which comprised 230 acres (92 hectares). It was 'commonly known by the name of Government Cottage and Garden or Farm at Strawberry Hill' and was officially valued at £206.14.0.

Additions in wattle and daub were made to the original dwelling, sheds and stables were built, ditches dug, hedges planted and sheep and cattle bought. In 1836 a contract was signed with William Diprose for the building of a two-storey stone house. The contract sum was £100 but this appears to have been for labour only.

Much of the material was brought from England which explains why Diprose's contract may have been for labour only. Stone was the main local content. Doors, windows, flooring and roofing slates were all imported.

The internal walls were built in an old English style known as brick nogging or half-timbered — a timber frame with brick infilling.

Further additions were made from time to time, in stone and in timber. An unusual feature is a stone holding tank into which water was pumped from an underground spring or soak.

Seeds, fruit trees and plants were also brought out by the Spencers, as well as furniture and furnishings. It all gave the house and surroundings the appearance of a 'little bit of England'.

Sir Richard Spencer died in 1839, but the estate was carried on by Lady Spencer and some of her sons — there were six sons and three daughters in the family. In 1843 she departed for England, taking her three youngest sons with her for further schooling. During her three year absence the farm was occupied by George Egerton-Warburton, who had married the youngest Spencer girl, Augusta.

After Lady Spencer's death the farm was worked by the eldest remaining son, Edward, until he died in 1869. It appears to have been mainly untenanted from that date. In 1870 the original wattle and daub cottage was destroyed

R.A.Smolicz '82

Old Strawberry Hill Farm

ALBANY (1836)

by fire. The remaining buildings and farm gradually deteriorated, once used as a Chinese garden and then a slaughterhouse.

A reprieve came in 1889 when the property was purchased by a young Perth architect, Francis Bird. He moved his practice to Albany and his family to the Old Farm, which he restored. Bird died in 1937, his wife in 1946. A second period of neglect and deterioration then commenced.

Finally, after being purchased by the Western Australian Government in 1956, the house was vested in the Albany Town Council in 1961 and transferred to the National Trust in 1963. The Trust has now restored the main building and it is once more virtually as originally built.

Where there was a water supply in the form of a well or holding cistern, a pump was required to raise the water. Several variations of this type were imported from England.

VICTORIA

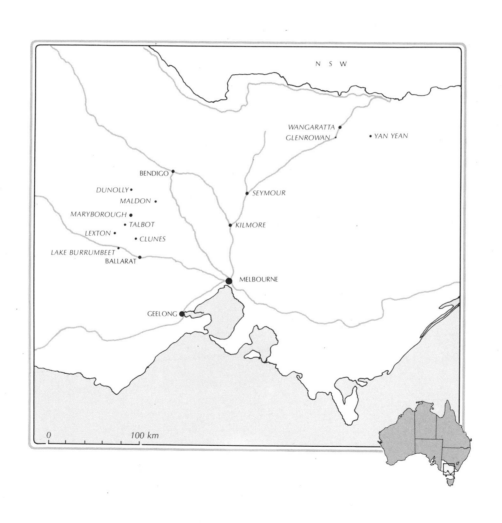

N S W

WANGARATTA •
GLENROWAN •   • YAN YEAN

BENDIGO •

DUNOLLY •
MALDON •   • SEYMOUR

MARYBOROUGH •
LEXTON •   • TALBOT
         • CLUNES   • KILMORE

LAKE BURRUMBEET
BALLARAT •

                              ● MELBOURNE

GEELONG ●

0   100 km

Bear's Castle

YAN YEAN,
Victoria

1840

Shelters made of earth used in various ways — adobe, pisé, mud brick — are probably second in age only to natural caves. Even today experiments are being carried out in the use, development and potential of this technique.

Records go back to 8000 BC in Mesopotamia where bricks of earth were shaped by hand and dried in the sun and then laid in a mortar of mud. Some 4000 years later a mould was invented and the brick assumed something of the shape it enjoys today, with uniformity of size and reasonably sharp edges.

With such a long history it is not surprising that here and there one comes across examples of earth dwellings surviving from Australia's pioneering days. It was only that bark or slab huts could be erected so much more quickly that they were used more often.

Bear's Castle, as it is now called, built at Yan Yean in Victoria in 1840, is a well preserved example of an early earth dwelling with many unique features giving it a more than usual interest. It is a square building, two storeys high, with walls built of cob strengthened with a circular buttress at each corner.

Cob consists of a mixture of clay and straw, packed and rammed until it becomes strong and durable. The two-storey walls of this material probably would not have been stable without the unique buttresses.

The footings and lower part of the walls are of undressed stones of all shapes and sizes, laid in clay mortar and brought up to a reasonably level finish. On this was laid the cob, placed in layers or courses.

One of the buttresses contains a rammed earth circular staircase leading to the first floor, while another is built up in stone and clay and is a fireplace and chimney flue. The first floor is constructed of logs laid close together and covered with a thick layer of clay forced down to key into the intervening spaces.

The roof is framed up in the conventional way with sapling rafters and is covered with thatch. The supports for door and window openings are far from conventional. They are tree forks, standing upside down and built in as the walls were shaped around them.

This is perhaps the simplest form of mud or clay construction, but several variations were and are used. Blocks are cast in moulds and can be made up of several mixtures of mud or clay and straw, grass, or even sticks, or with clay alone if it is of suitable consistency.

An alternative is earth rammed between forming, rising about 600 millimetres at a time. The builder works right around all the walls so that no part advances faster than the rest. Window and door openings can be made as the work proceeds, using forming, or can be cut out afterwards.

Post and beam construction is another alternative. A frame with corner posts and others at strategic points such as door and window openings, and beams connecting all the posts at the top, is first built. Then the roof is framed up and covered, allowing work to proceed under it in all weathers. Finally the walls of cob or rammed earth are built as filling between posts.

Bear's Castle

YAN YEAN (1840)

Kelly Cottage

GLENROWAN,
Victoria

1840s

The town of Glenrowan, in Victoria, was made famous by the exploits and later the final siege of the Kelly gang of bushrangers.

The story begins with the transportation to Tasmania of John Kelly for attempting to shoot his landlord. When his sentence expired Kelly moved to Victoria, where he settled at Wareen, 60 kilometres from Melbourne. He set up a horse stealing business, taking the horses through the rough hilly country to what is now the New South Wales border and selling them in the Murray Valley area.

His activities led him into territory already claimed by a stronger band of horse stealers, who naturally resented this intrusion. One night they captured John Kelly and his family, along with another family named Quinn who at times collaborated with the Kellys.

The Kellys and Quinns were taken to the top of a nearby range and ordered to stay north of it on pain of death. Choosing the lesser of two evils they moved north and settled near what is now the town of Glenrowan.

The Kelly cottage at Glenrowan purports to be the original but it is more likely a replica. As far as can be established it is an exact copy of the original and is now a main tourist attraction in the town.

John Kelly had seven children, quite a crowd to accommodate in such a small dwelling, but that was not unusual in those days. He died in 1865 and his family, or part of it, carried on the horse stealing business.

The best known of his children, Edward or Ned, became an accomplice of a bushranger named Harry Power, but it was not long before both were arrested. However, Ned gave an indication of his character by turning Queen's Evidence and testifying against his mate, Power, thus earning, or at least receiving, a pardon.

Not long afterwards he formed the gang whose exploits have become, with many embellishments, firmly established in Australian folklore.

The Kelly cottage is typical of the dwellings of the time. There are solid ground plates at the foot of each wall with posts set into them at intervals. Posts were also set on each side of the door and window openings and at the corners and intersections. Split slabs were dropped into channels in the plates and another plate set at the top of the walls.

The roof was made with sapling rafters, with lighter saplings secured across them to carry the bark covering. A ridge capping of bark made the roof watertight. The bark was further held in place by fairly heavy saplings laid over it and pegged or wired in place.

The front of the house features what became the ubiquitous veranda, matched by a skillion section at the rear which housed wash room and other ancillary rooms.

Veranda posts and the plate they carry are round.

Kelly Cottage

GLENROWAN (1840s)

Wattle and Daub Hut

LEXTON,
Victoria

1850s

The dwelling pictured is one of the oldest in Victoria. It is a very crude example of what became known as wattle and daub or wattle and dab construction.

As with most of these very early homes there is only one room, measuring in this case 2.7 metres by 2.5 metres. There are stringybark sapling posts at each corner with another midway along each wall.

Centre posts at the gable ends extend above the ridge line. A plate at the top of each side wall is of the same material, as are the rafters of the simple gable roof.

There is one door and two window openings of about 400 millimetres square. The roof is covered with bark from a stringybark tree.

Much smaller saplings or branches of 35 to 50 millimetres in diameter are secured over the posts and the intervening spaces filled with river mud with a high sand content. Inside the walls are covered with newspaper.

This method of construction was often used by the early settlers and was a development of the old English practice of wattling. There, slender whippy tree branches were laced within a frame to construct hurdles, which were connected together in various ways to make temporary fences.

Trees with branches suitable for wattling were found quite close to Sydney Cove. By a natural progression these trees were given the name of wattle and later, because of the dark colour of the bark, black wattle. This name was perpetuated by Blackwattle Bay at Glebe in Sydney. Later the *Acacia* family of trees was given the common name of wattle.

However, the trees generally used for wattle and daub are not wattles at all, but *Callicoma serratifolia*, a relative of the Christmas bush.

In front of this wattle and daub hut is a second house built either when the first began to deteriorate, or when circumstances permitted the erection of a more lasting and comfortable dwelling. This is a more or less conventional timber frame structure sheathed on the outside with lapped boards and on the inside with dressed tongue and groove timber linings.

The roof, originally shingles placed in a highly unusual herring-bone pattern, is now covered with corrugated iron. The two chimneys are built of hand-made bricks.

The two houses are not far from Lexton and clearly visible just off the Beaufort Road. The current owner is Mr Frank Briody.

The dwelling standing immediately in front of the wattle and daub house is of a later vintage and orthodox construction. It has not withstood the ravages of time and neglect much better than the older one.

Wattle and Daub Hut

LEXTON (1850s)

Stone Dwelling

DUNOLLY,

Victoria

1860s

There is a small stone dwelling just near one of the roads between Dunolly and Bendigo that has many points of interest. However, little appears to be known about it.

Although not very far from Bendigo, Dunolly was not within the richest goldfields area. Some fossickers did work the area but it is unlikely that this was a gold miner's dwelling. Most of these were built in a hurry and were of a more temporary nature.

There is evidence of some haste in the building although the stone construction suggests an intention of permanent occupation. The stones in the first few courses are dressed and laid in a rough ashlar pattern. This gives way to the speedier erection of rubble up to the eaves line on the two lower walls. A return to ashlar work for the top courses of the gable ends ensured a better finish. It also made a level bed for the timber plates of the upper part of the gables which are filled with timber framing and horizontal boarding.

As was fairly usual at the time the sapling rafters are tied with joists nearly a metre above the plate line, giving the effect of a coved ceiling. It also reduced the amount of material required for the walls.

There are window openings in the end walls and these probably did not contain frames or sashes as a rough lean-to structure at each end gives them protection from the weather.

The main roof and that of each lean-to is covered with bark.

Although this is a relatively dry part of Victoria, general farming was carried out in the area around this dwelling. Now it is a piggery and this former dwelling is used to house some of the animals.

The more modern homestead nearby, although obviously more comfortable and well fitted up, is not built of such enduring materials as this old dwelling and it is quite likely that the stone walls will still be standing after the newer building has gone.

Not far away at Dunolly is one of the largest wheat silos in the world with most of the grain grown to the west of this agriculture centre and railhead.

RA Smolicz '81.

Stone Dwelling

DUNOLLY (1860s)

St Paul's Church of England Church

CLUNES,

Victoria

1860

The first Church of England service to be held in Victoria took place in a barn on the Henty property at Portland in 1834. Development was relatively slow in the Colony and was centred on the Port Phillip area for a long time.

The authorities discouraged spreading out into the hinterland. They found it difficult to provide protection for the settlers from the unruly among the white population and the disgruntled Aborigines.

The discovery of gold was to cause an increase in population and a spread that the authorities could not control. A William Campbell is believed to have first found gold at Clunes as early as 1850, but its discovery was not reported until James Esmonds took samples to Geelong in July 1851.

The gold at Clunes was in quartz reefs. Esmonds brought some iron back from Melbourne, and with a joiner named Pugh, made a cradle. The pair thus became the first to mine gold in Victoria.

A rush to Clunes followed but many of the would-be miners were disappointed as the gold was difficult to recover without machinery.

In the meantime alluvial gold was discovered at Ballarat, Castlemaine and several other towns, so Clunes did not develop as a town, but remained a collection of tents and huts.

By 1857 two large companies, the Port Phillip and Colonial Gold Mining Company and the Clunes Quartz Mining Company were formed. They brought in machinery and mining was commenced on a large scale, heralding the real development of the district.

The first recorded church service in Clunes was held in 1855 under a large gum tree which stood on some flat ground in Lower Fraser Street. The first service under cover appears to have been held some time later in the blacksmith shop of the Port Phillip and Colonial Gold Mining Company. In 1857 the Wesleyan community erected a small timber chapel in Fraser Street.

The first Anglican church was erected in Fraser Street in 1860, mainly through the efforts of the resident director of the Port Phillip and Colonial Gold Mining Company. Nine years later this was moved to Templeton Street where it now stands and is used as a Sunday School.

The first site in Fraser Street was sold for £714 and this started the building fund for the imposing bluestone church of St Paul which now stands in Templeton Street.

The addition of a transept enlarged the original church building (now Sunday School). It is a simply designed, white painted wooden structure with a corrugated galvanised iron roof.

Unpretentious, its pleasing proportions give it a charm not always found in more elaborate structures. An unusual feature is the use of label moulds over the square-headed window and door openings. It was actually a device to divert rainwater from running down the facade. The moulds are continued for an appropriate distance down each side of the reveals. Although purely a practical feature, they give the building an individual character.

St Paul's Church of England Church

CLUNES (1860)

Methodist Church

TALBOT,

Victoria

1862

The story of Talbot follows that of so many of the towns in Victoria and New South Wales that bloomed almost overnight in the great gold era of Australia's history. Some of them, such as Bathurst in New South Wales and Ballarat and Bendigo in Victoria, have grown into provincial cities. But Talbot, like the vast majority, has slipped back into a sleepy country town, the bustling life of a boom town giving way once more to peaceful tranquillity.

Talbot came to life as the centre of a sheep farming area, the first grazing lease of 63,360 acres (25,640 hectares) being granted to Alexander McCallum in 1848.

The first official discovery of gold was made in 1852 but there were probably a number of earlier finds. It is known that a shepherd named Thomas Chapman made a find at least one year earlier, but early discoveries were usually kept secret, often for fear of prosecution.

Thirty turbulent years followed with amazing yields of gold. Talbot developed into a township boasting a population of 3400 at its peak.

There were at least six streets of stores and business premises, their names reflecting the origins of the inhabitants. Scandinavian Crescent speaks for itself. There were even Bond, Oxford and Russell Streets.

A history of Talbot records 23 restaurants, a variety of hotels and ale stores, tobacconists, four butchers, five boot shops or bootmakers, three tent shops, six drapers, a number of druggists or chemist shops, milliners, saddlers, confectioners and billiard saloons in the Crescent alone. Prominent among the service industries in the town was the Talbot Coach Factory, makers of buggies, dog-carts, carry-alls, phaetons, spring carts, chaises and drays.

The town was well served with churches as well as a court house, borough offices, two breweries, a soap and candle factory and 16 hotels.

A Presbyterian church was built in Heales Street in 1864. The following year saw St Michael's Church of England, a Roman Catholic church, a Methodist church and a Primitive Methodist church — a much stricter sect of Methodism.

There were a number of followers of John Wesley among the miners. These people erected churches, mainly of canvas, which could be easily dismantled and moved to new sites as the mining community moved from place to place.

As the Talbot community became more settled a permanent site in Camp Street was acquired for a Methodist Church and Thomas Taggard built the substantial place of worship pictured here for the sum of £525. The foundation stone was laid on 22 December 1862 and the first service held on 29 March of the following year.

The twin spires give the building a unique and interesting appearance. They emphasise the symmetry of the main street front, framing a lancet-arched entrance with double doors. There is an impressive three light and rose window above it. Along each side of the building are five narrow lancet-headed windows with buttresses between.

Methodist Church

TALBOT (1862)

Oswald's Cottage

MALDON,
Victoria

1860s

In November 1853 a Captain Mechosk made a gold strike on the slopes of Mount Tarrangower. Mount Tarrangower is just to the west of what is now the township of Maldon, notable among other things for being the geographic centre of Victoria. More importantly it is regarded by the National Trust as the 'best preserved town in Australia of the gold mining era'.

The creeks and valleys of the district were rich in alluvial gold. Large mounds resulting from the diggings are still to be seen just outside the town.

Quartz mining followed and this gave the town its real impetus. A 488 metre-long tunnel (Carmen's Tunnel), carved out of solid bluestone, is a tourist attraction.

Over two million ounces (56,700 kg) of gold were officially recorded as having been recovered at Maldon. There must have been considerably more taken but not recorded.

A prosperous town soon replaced the tents and shanties of the early miners. Firstly there were small cottages of stone and logs or split slabs. Later quite substantial buildings, some with architectural merit, resulted in a town of more than usual historical interest.

Also many old world trees and shrubs were introduced and these, while to some extent taking away the typically Australian atmosphere, are in harmony with the nineteenth century buildings. It is claimed that no other town in Victoria has such a varied collection of European trees.

The old market place is now a museum displaying many interesting relics of Maldon's past. On the sites of some of the mines are quartz kilns and crushers, cyanide vats and puddling machines.

There are many old cottages still in reasonable repair, some still lived in. Pictured is Oswald's cottage, in High Street. At first glance one would think it was intended for Pygmies, the walls and doors being less than two metres in height. But, as in many old English cottages, the ceiling is coved, the joists occurring some distance up the rafters.

The walls are of an early type of weatherboard, the roof originally shingled.

Oswald's Cottage

MALDON (1860s)

Cobb & Co. Inn

TALBOT,

Victoria

1870

On the outskirts of the Victorian town of Talbot, on the road to Clunes, are the remains of the first inn to be built in the district. It was a regular stopping place for Cobb & Co. coaches.

The building is disappearing fast as the materials, especially the bricks, are being used in the construction of a cottage on the same property.

The first migrants to any new land naturally follow, as nearly as possible, the construction methods used in the country of their origin. It is usually two or more generations later before differences of climate and the unavailability of familiar materials lead to the development of new and more suitable building practices.

Thus it is not remarkable that this early building was built in a way closely resembling the Tudor half-timbered work of sixteenth and seventeenth century England.

Here a timber frame of plates and studs was erected and then the spaces between the studs filled with hand-made bricks. Hoop iron straps nailed to the studs and carried across the brickwork every few courses tied bricks and timber together.

The local hand-made bricks proved much more porous than those of England and unable to keep out the heavier rain of the new country. To remedy this defect rough sawn boards overlapping like modern weatherboard were nailed across the studs over the brickwork, resulting in a solid and weatherproof structure.

There are other similarly constructed buildings in the Talbot district, although only a few remains are still in existence.

The interior walls of the old inn were also timber-framed, infilled with brick. They were then plastered over, either at the time of building or later. When 110 millimetre studs were used the bricks were laid flat and with the thinner 75 millimetre studs they were placed on their edge. A rock lime mortar was used.

Roof construction was conventional with a covering of shingles. The flooring was Baltic pine and the ceilings of imported pressed decorative metal panels.

It was possible to step from the road straight into the bar with its three-sided counter. There was a cellar directly under the barman's working space.

When demolition started an English penny bearing the date 1873 was found on top of one of the walls, giving an approximate indication of the time of building.

A separate entrance door led into the residential section of the inn, which provided for the innkeeper's family and very little in the way of guest accommodation.

Cobb & Co. Inn

TALBOT (1870)

Ercildoun

LAKE BORRUMBEET,
Victoria

c. 1840

*Original Learmonth
dwelling, Ercildoun*

Two seafaring adventurers, the Learmonth brothers, arrived in Australia from the border country of Scotland in 1837 and explored the country around Buninyong and Mount Misery in southern Victoria. The next year they returned and selected a large area near Lake Borrumbeet, naming their selection Borrumbeet Run.

This name was later discarded for Ercildoun, a phonetic rendering of Earlston, where their Scottish ancestors had lived for centuries.

Apparently plenty of labour was available to the Learmonths for they planned an extensive stone mansion. First, they had a temporary home built, in which they lived while the larger homestead was under construction.

The original house is built on steeply sloping ground. It is on two levels, one entered from the high side, the other separately from the lower level. The lower portion is built of hard, local granite or bluestone, laid mostly as random rubble, the upper courses roughly squared. This portion consisted of an earth-floored living room and kitchen. The upper storey was the dayroom, the walls framed up and with slabs split into rough boards placed between the studs. The floor is of timber.

The brothers moved to the lower floor at night and barred themselves in, a precaution considered necessary as by that time the white settlers had antagonised the Aborigines, who had learned to retaliate. Also several of the released transported prisoners had taken to bushranging.

There is no record of the time taken to build

the main homestead but such a large building must have occupied a great number of men for many months. A number if not all of the tradesmen employed were skilled. The hard local granite was expertly worked to result in immaculate ashlar work.

It is doubtful if the building was properly or completely planned. It is an architectural curiosity and has every appearance of having 'just grown'. There is a strange mixture of styles and periods, with Scottish Baronial being the overriding impression. Inscribed into the keystone over the main entrance arch is the date 1837.

Inside there is an air of grandeur. It is possible that parquet floors and similar features were added at various times. Certainly an additional suite was built to accommodate the Duke of Gloucester, who stayed there for several days in 1934.

The circular well over the entrance hall, with its central chandelier, is the most outstanding feature of the interior and was obviously there from the beginning.

Situated a few kilometres off the highway which links Melbourne and Adelaide, the house has had few owners. Sometime after 1872 the Learmonths sold the property to Samuel (later Sir Samuel) Wilson, a member of the Victorian legislative assembly. They had been through the disastrous drought of 1872 and later the indignity of being held up by a bushranger.

The Learmonths had laid out a garden of 13 acres (five hectares) to provide a setting for the homestead and planted it with Scottish trees,

Ercildoun

LAKE BORRUMBEET (c. 1840)

shrubs and flowers. Sir Samuel Wilson walled in an area of one acre (about half a hectare) around the house and made a more intimate garden. He enclosed another 300 acres (120 hectares) with a slab fence, nearly three metres high, to contain a large herd of deer.

The house remained vacant for some time after Sir Samuel left for England. (He had been born in Ireland.) During part of this period it was leased by Dame Nellie Melba.

Eventually the property was purchased by Sir Alan Currie and the house came to life again.

The Curries played host to a large number of distinguished guests and carried out many improvements to the property itself. Sir Alan Currie was a breeder of bloodstock — horses, sheep and cattle.

Among the improvements were several large dams and, most spectacular of all, a long open concrete channel to bring water to a large stone tank. The tank filled during the day and at night the water was utilised to drive a turbine which generated electricity for the homestead.

The house was again vacant for some years after the death of Sir Alan Currie until it was purchased by the present owners, the five Briody brothers.

The property is now run very efficiently for grazing but the house is only occupied by caretakers, Mr and Mrs Austin O'Malley. They have devoted a great deal of time and energy to restoring both house and furniture and to maintaining both in an immaculate condition.

SOUTH AUSTRALIA

PORT AUGUSTA

WILMINGTON

ORROROO

WHYALLA

PORT PIRIE

Burra

Clare

POLISH HILL RIVER

KADINA

AUBURN

Spencer Gulf

ADELAIDE

Gulf Saint Vincent

0   100 km

Mine Executive's Cottage

KADINA,
South Australia

1848

A party of troops sent from Sydney Town sailed into St Vincent's Gulf, South Australia, and planted the Union Flag on Kangaroo Island in 1836, thus completing Great Britain's claim to the whole continent.

Settlement in the area was understandably slow until the discovery of copper ore in 1844. The mining and smelting of copper is not in the province of the small fossicker so it was necessary for companies with sufficient capital to be formed. This led to a demand for labour to work in the mines and the smelters. Much of this labour was imported from Cornwall, where experienced miners were readily available, and from Wales to work in the smelters.

Towns grew up around the mines — cottages, hotels and shops were built by the mining companies. At Kadina most of the miners built their own homes. They were crude structures of whatever materials were at hand and most have long since collapsed into a heap of rubble.

The company also built dwellings for its supervisors and executives. Most of these consisted of four rooms, in a simple rectangle, with a veranda in front. An example of one is pictured.

Later another large room, called a villa, was added at each end of the original structure. With much higher ceilings these additions dominated the buildings and overshadowed the original sections.

Walls were constructed of stone, laid in random rubble with squared quoin stones. They were half a metre thick. The villas at each end were built as separate structures, again with walls half a metre thick, butting up against the original. Openings were cut from the new rooms into the older ones so that the walls here were a metre thick, the openings finished with splayed reveals.

The stones were laid in a pug mortar and rendered inside with a lime mortar. The ceilings were lined with ripple iron — sheets pressed into very small corrugations and known locally as 'fluke'.

The floors of the original portion of the cottage were an ash and clay mixture whereas the villas had timber floors. Each had a large fireplace, framed in carved timber and lined with hand painted Victorian tiles.

The life of most of the South Australian copper towns was a little more than 30 years. Their closing brought an end to an era of prosperity, of boom towns with hospitals, churches and the other imposing buildings that go with such circumstances.

The executive houses, in the row now called Stirling Terrace, in Kadina were sold for £25 each. The house pictured in the Terrace is the home of an artist, Ben Paech.

The Cornish character of this part of Yorke Peninsula comes to life again during a week in May each alternate year when Kadina, Wallaroo and Moonta celebrate the Kernewek Lowender Festival. Wheelbarrow races, street dancing, Cornish pasties and the special brew called 'Swanky' transform the area once again into 'Little Cornwall'.

Mine Executive's Cottage

KADINA (1848)

Yudnapinna Homestead

PORT AUGUSTA,

South Australia

c. 1850

Spencer's Gulf penetrates from the sea into the land mass of South Australia northwards for some 320 kilometres. It reaches to the 32nd parallel of latitude almost in line with Broken Hill in New South Wales.

Matthew Flinders reached the head of the Gulf in 1802, but very little further exploration took place until Edward John Eyre passed through in 1839 on his way to Mount Arden. Many attempts to settle in the district followed but it was 10 years or more before any real progress was made.

A town finally developed to provide a shipping terminal for wool and copper ore from the north. Situated on the east side near the head of the Gulf, it was named Port Augusta after the wife of the Deputy Governor.

A second town later grew on the western side of the Gulf. It was known as Port Augusta West. The two existed as quite separate communities until 1927 when a bridge was built across the Gulf.

The first settler in Port Augusta West was John McCarthy, a ferryman. When settlement developed he ferried fresh water in casks and the mail across the Gulf. He saved a long journey around the swampy ground at the headwaters of the Gulf to an old camel crossing 11 kilometres north of the town.

Some 80 kilometres north-west of Port Augusta is Yudnapinna Station, at one time the largest sheep station in South Australia. It achieved a record shearing of 100,000 sheep during the 1880s.

Yudnapinna was first leased to Mr T. McT. Gibson and Archdeacon Morse and it was during their tenancy that the pictured homestead was built. It is now the only pine log homestead still in existence in the State.

In 1975 the building was dismantled, transported 80 kilometres, and re-erected log by log in Homestead Park, Port Augusta, and is now used as a museum.

It is quite extensive and roofed in three different sections with the equivalent of the modern box gutter between. These three hipped roofs, together with the encircling veranda roof, are covered in shingles.

Walls are constructed with vertical logs at intervals, at corners, intersections and beside all openings. Shorter logs have been dropped in between. The inside finish is the same, the rounded logs giving an interesting and irregular pattern to the wall surfaces.

Roof water is collected and diverted into a stone-lined well. It is covered with a shingled roof which serves the triple purpose of safeguarding against accidents, keeping the water cool and preventing evaporation.

Yudnapinna Homestead

PORT AUGUSTA (c. 1850)

Bakery and Dwelling

AUBURN,
South Australia

1856

Burra, in South Australia, grew from a sleepy village to a fairly important township after the opening up of copper mining in the Burra Burra district in 1845. The discovery of copper by two shepherds, Thomas Pickett and William Streair, caused the formation of two mining syndicates. They were the Princess Royal Mining Association, known by the irreverent colonials as the Nobs, and the South Australian Mining Association, the Snobs.

This was followed by the migration of miners from Cornwall and smelterers from Wales and Germany.

The mined ore was transported by bullock waggon to Port Adelaide and Port Wakefield. A stopping place roughly half way along the route to Port Wakefield was established at Auburn and so the little town prospered.

One of the many buildings that were erected in response to the new trade was a shop and dwelling, pictured, on a corner of the main street. Built in 1855, the first owners were Miss McDonald and Mr East.

Originally there were four rooms and a bakery, built with stone walls half a metre thick and roofed with shingles. The interior doors were only 1.8 metres high, suggesting a Welsh influence.

Flooring was slate slabs, some of them up to two metres long, from Mintaro Quarry in the Clare Valley. Ceilings were varied, some of ripple iron or 'fluke'. Heavy iron hooks built into the ceiling in one room were used for hanging the family meat supply.

The large fireplace chimneys are a feature of the outside of the building.

The small paned windows of the shop are typical of the period and give a pleasant character to the building. The veranda not only shades and protects the walls of the shop and the goods displayed but also provides a welcome resting place for weary travellers.

After the first owners had gone Mr Isaac Meller had some additions made to the building. He built up a flourishing business, enlarging the bakery into a general store. He catered for almost everything the bullock drivers and other travellers would need.

The shop is now occupied by a fruiterer, the present owner being Mrs Jean E. Glover, a daughter of Isaac Meller. The building has been classified by the National Trust of South Australia.

Bakery and Dwelling

AUBURN (1856)

Boundary Rider's Dwelling

WILMINGTON,
South Australia

c. 1860

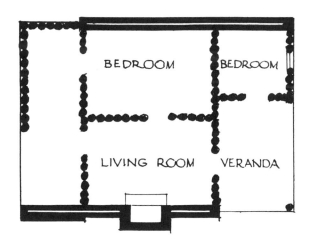

Various parts of Australia were settled as a result of people fleeing from religious or political persecution in Europe. It was natural that groups of such migrants remained together and established what became ethnic communities. In some cases they were not well received by other and earlier migrants who were anxious to leave old differences behind and establish a more tolerant society in the new land.

Lutherans from Germany and Austria were the best known of these religious groups, but Polish Hill River in South Australia tells of refugees from Poland who arrived in 1870. There were 200 of them, their leader an ex-naval officer.

Mount Brown Station occupied a large area of land on the outskirts of the present town of Wilmington. A small part of this station was bought in 1900 by Mr Modystach, one of the early Polish migrants. On it was the boundary rider's cottage pictured here, described at the time as being 'very old'.

It is now the property of John Modystach, a great grandson of the first owner.

The end walls of the cottage are stone, laid as rubble in a mud mortar. They are unique in that they are of cavity construction.

Cavity walls were developed in Australia when it was found that the local clay produced a brick that was not watertight. The heavier rain quickly penetrated the solid brick walls built in the English system so a double skin with a cavity in the middle soon became the norm. It was very unusual, however, to adopt this system for stone walls.

The longer walls are of vertical timber slabs, shaped to fit into plates at the top and bottom. The spaces between slabs are packed with mud on the inside only.

The roof is framed up with round timbers and covered with corrugated galvanised iron. It may originally have been shingled or thatched. The ceilings are lined with heavy sail cloth.

The veranda is also framed up with round timbers and covered with corrugated galvanised iron. Floors are rammed earth.

Boundary Rider's Dwelling

WILMINGTON (c. 1860)

Polish Church

POLISH HILL RIVER,
South Australia

1870s

Window heads were spanned in various ways, usually with a single stone lintel. Where a suitable stone was not available, as at Polish Hill River, a lintel was made up of two head stones, with a keystone wedged in the centre.

The history of Poland is a long story of oppression, exploitation, partition and revolts. In the period 1830 to the First World War the country was divided into three parts controlled by Russia, Prussia and Austria. There was also religious persecution, as many Poles objected to the form of Lutheranism forced on them by the Prussians and the Austrians. One result of all this was a fairly constant migration to various parts of the world.

In 1869 a number of Poles settled around Sevenhill East in South Australia, near the source of the Hill River. The place became known as Polish Hill River.

Their numbers were augmented by a party of about 200 who arrived in early 1870 under the charge of an ex-naval officer named Gerke.

They brought with them a number of grape cuttings and soon had vineyards established.

At first they lacked religious guidance for although there was a strong Catholic settlement nearby at Sevenhill, no priest spoke Polish. But in April, 1870, a Father Rogaleski arrived and immediately set about building a church.

Such was the enthusiasm of the Poles that the building was completed by the end of November in the same year, mostly with materials found ready to hand.

Six years previously the Jesuits at Sevenhill had begun to build St Aloysius', a much more ambitious project, but work stopped after two years for lack of funds. Building was resumed immediately after the Polish church was finished and according to Jesuit records it could not have been completed in the four years without the community spirit of their Polish neighbours.

The Poles supplied voluntary labour for their church, cutting and carting building stone and slate. The arches and trusses that carry the roof were cut by them from the giant red gums, known as Clare red gums, a particular species not known anywhere else in Australia.

The design of the church is simple, four square and uncompromising, reflecting the character of its builders. The stone is squared and laid in courses with impressive quoins or corner stones, each two courses in height.

Window reveals are treated in the same way. The sills are each one long stone while the heads are spanned with two stones. There is a wedge-shaped keystone in the centre.

142

Polish Church

POLISH HILL RIVER (1870s)

The porch is slightly disproportionate but this minor blemish goes unnoticed as it manages to fit into the general character of the building.

Although the church is the best known building of this Polish community, their stone cottages are equally characteristic.

One of these, pictured, is quite close to the church. Its stone walls bear evidence of much hastier erection, but they are just as sound and substantial. The stone was not squared but laid as rubble with very strong corner stones or quoins and some rough coursing, especially approaching the eaves.

The plan consists of two rooms, the larger a combined living area and kitchen, the smaller a bedroom. There is a veranda across the main front, probably a later addition. A feature of the larger room is a massive corner fireplace, serving the combined purposes of cooking, baking and heating.

Many of the people now living at Polish Hill River are descendants of the original Polish migrants and their vineyards are still producing high quality wines. Their vines are propagated from those brought out from Poland more than 150 years ago.

Polish Hill River Cottage

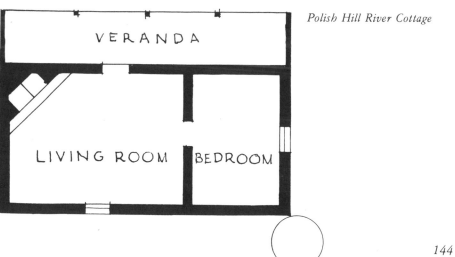

144

NORTHERN TERRITORY

ELCHO ISLAND

DARWIN

NHULUNBUY (GOVE)

KATHERINE

ROPER BAR

MATARANKA

0   200 km

Springvale Station

KATHERINE,
Northern Territory

1877

John McDouall Stuart, a hardy Scot from Fifeshire, who was then a draughtsman in the Government Surveyor's employ, and John Harris-Browne, a surgeon, were among the members of Charles Sturt's party during the latter's epic exploration in 1844.

The draughtsman and the doctor made later trips right across the continent and after one of these Harris-Browne told his brother, Dr William Browne, who already had several cattle stations in the north of South Australia, that he believed there was the potential for successful sheep and cattle raising in the far north.

In 1876 Dr William Browne took out a lease on 1163 square miles (3012 square kilometres) of country near Katherine, some 240 kilometres south of Port Darwin. He then sent Alfred Giles, who knew something of the country through his involvement with the Overland Telegraph Line, to drive 12,000 head of sheep and 4000 head of cattle from Port Augusta to his holding and to establish a homestead there.

The party comprised 40 men and 90 horses. Experiencing drought, flood, poison bush and a dry stage of 150 kilometres, the successful achievement of this venture is still regarded as an epic droving feat.

Giles had arranged for and paid for fresh supplies of food to be awaiting him at the Katherine Telegraph Station, but through some 'misunderstanding' all that was there when he arrived was two tons of weevily flour.

For the homestead he selected a site on the Katherine River where there was an abundance of water and a fine view and suggested the name Springvale. He set those of his men who were not suffering from malaria to work and by the time the wet season arrived the buildings were well under way. They comprised a manager's house, men's quarters, blacksmith shop, some sheds and a store, a horse paddock and stock yards.

Although most of these buildings were of timber — split slabs in the main — and have succumbed to the ravages of time and a harsh climate, those that were stone remain. They were of limestone quarried nearby under the direction of the chief stonemason whose name, appropriately, was Fred Stone. Their sturdy construction and utilitarian design portray the needs and attitudes of the time.

There was a ready market for the products of the station for some years. The Overland Telegraph, the growing town of Palmerston and the gold rush at Pine Creek all contributed to a period of prosperity.

But more stations were established in the surrounding country and the competition for what had become a declining market increased when the gold rush subsided. This so affected Springvale's profitability that it was not a commercial proposition, although it was operated as recently as 1976.

The present owners, Katherine Gorge Tourist Agency, under the management of Brian Lambert, co-operating with the National Trust of Australia, are restoring those buildings that can be saved. They have built other accommodation and have developed the property as a tourist centre, while retaining as much of the original atmosphere as possible.

Springvale Station

KATHERINE (1877)

Old St Mary's Star of the Sea Church

DARWIN,

Northern Territory

1882

After several abortive attempts to establish a main centre in the north of Australia, Port Darwin was finally selected in 1868 and the town — then called Palmerston — was surveyed. Later the name was changed to Darwin.

On 12 July 1882 a ship named the *Meath* called at Port Darwin. On board were two priests on their way from France to New Guinea. They landed and on the following morning baptised three children, one being the child of the director of the Electric Telegraph Station. This was the first recorded activity of the Roman Catholic Church in Darwin.

It was followed by the establishment of a mission station, the first Mass being said in a house in Bennett Street. Very soon afterwards the Jesuits built a church in Smith Street.

The design of this early building is evidence that already the Jesuits had an appreciation of the needs of the strange tropical climate, so different from that of their homeland. Verandas on three sides provided much needed shade. The walls were of timber slabs slotted into square posts and the windows — designed in a simplification of Gothic arches — were larger than was usual in those days.

The most striking feature was the bell tower, which consisted of the main trunk of a tree which forked some three metres from the ground, providing two vertical members in which to place the bell. Two pieces of sawn hardwood were used as stabilising struts.

The priests were stationed at an Aboriginal mission at Rapid Creek, necessitating a 10 kilometre walk to and from Darwin every Sunday to conduct services.

Sixteen years after it was built the original church of St Mary's was flattened in a cyclone, the bell tower being the only portion left standing. The church was rebuilt to a similar plan, with some additional buttressing and some simplification of details, such as the omission of the veranda brackets which represented seagulls.

Additions in the form of transepts and a new sanctuary were made in 1920, using timber from Bathurst Island.

The tranquil life of Darwin Parish and the several mission stations that had been built up within its jurisdiction was suddenly shattered in 1942 when Japanese bombs first fell on Australian soil. Darwin was transformed into a military town, complete with army chaplains.

Almost overnight the church became too small as troops flocked to it for Mass, but this problem was overcome by a group of army engineers who moved the walls of the nave out to the edge of the veranda.

After the Second World War the town of Darwin grew rapidly. The need for a much larger church soon became evident and plans were laid for the building of a cathedral which was officially opened on 19 August 1962 and named in honour of its predecessor, St Mary's Star of the Sea.

The final chapter in the story of old St Mary's was written by Cyclone Tracy, which completely destroyed it on Christmas Day, 1974. The Cathedral was damaged during the same cyclone, but it has been restored.

Old St Mary's Star of the Sea Church

DARWIN (1882)

Roper Bar Police Station and Dwelling

ROPER BAR,

Northern Territory

1890

The Roper River flows roughly in an easterly direction, into the Gulf of Carpentaria. It was probably first seen by a white man when Ludwig Leichhardt, a German botanist and explorer, crossed it in 1845 during his expedition to find a route from Moreton Bay in Queensland to Port Essington in the Northern Territory.

He crossed it at a spot, now known as Roper Bar, which was to gain prominence during the building of the Overland Telegraph Line from north to south. It was here that supplies for the line were landed after having been brought by ship up the Roper River.

Roper Bar continued to function as a terminal point for shipping which served the outlying cattle stations until the paddle steamer, *The Young Australian*, was wrecked not far downstream in 1892.

The Overland Telegraph Line was the major achievement of its day, stretching for nearly 2900 kilometres, 2415 of them through practically unknown country. Its length had been traversed only once — by John McDouall Stuart's party in 1862.

Until 1872 there was a once-monthly mail service to Europe, carried by P & O ships. In 1870 the British-Australian Telegraph Company made an agreement with the South Australian Government to lay a cable from Port Darwin to Java, which was already connected to Europe, on condition that a land line was constructed across Australia.

A side effect of this mammoth undertaking was the opening up of much of the inland. Telegraph stations were built at intervals of about 320 kilometres. Graziers, realising that thousands of sheep and cattle were required to feed the workforce on the line, set up grazing properties right across the continent.

The police station was probably established in 1885, after attacks had been made on travellers on the overland route. The area around the Roper was considered a dangerous portion of the track. At first the police lived in tents but towards the end of the century a 'rough timber and corrugated iron structure' was built (see picture). The ubiquitous corrugated iron was by then established as the principal building material for outback Australia.

The residential quarters of the police station consisted of two living rooms, one providing accommodation for two white policemen, the other for five black trackers.

The building was shaded back and front by verandas, the roofs supported on slender iron posts and the floor consisted of stone slabs smoothed over with cement. It is still standing although not in continuous use.

Roper Bar Police Station and Dwelling

ROPER BAR (1890)

Elcho Island Church

ELCHO ISLAND,
Northern Territory

1900

In more than 30,000 years of living in Australia the Aborigines' life had been ordered by a very strict code. It determined religious beliefs, family and tribal life and morals. It ensured a comparatively peaceful co-existence within their own group and with their neighbours.

The courage, zeal and devotion of those missionaries who set out to displace such ancient beliefs and woo these people over to Christianity cannot be denied. Whether or not this zeal was misplaced is a question that will probably never be satisfactorily decided.

To add to the confusion in the Aborigines' minds on being told that age-old beliefs and customs were wrong was the fact that there were numerous different missionary groups in the field.

Fond of singing, the beautiful music of the new religion won over many converts. Where they had not been embittered by contact with the more unsavoury of the whites, they usually gave the missionaries a courteous welcome.

While Europeans envisage a church as the most pretentious building in a town or district, the Aborigines demonstrated that the appeal of a natural setting can be possibly even more appropriate. They listened to the ardent and dedicated missionary — mostly not understanding what he was saying — under the shade of a spreading tree, beside a sacred waterhole, or on some tribal meeting place.

While the Aborigines did not fully understand the missionary, he did not understand them either. He told them of the churches and great cathedrals in which white men worshipped their strange god. Eager to please, groups of Aborigines built their own versions of a white man's church in some places.

One such is at Elcho Island in the Northern Territory (see picture). There are no stone walls with gothic-arched windows, no stained glass, no lofty ceilings in which the sound of the human voice can be lost or distorted — none of the ritual trappings.

The materials came from the bush that surrounded the clearing in which the church stands. The result was a simple structure with bush poles for posts, plates and rafters. The roof was covered with long strips of bark and some rough poles were provided to sit on.

The church was built, almost certainly, just to please one earnest white man, himself harassed by an unfriendly government as much as the Aborigines were. There may be more to be gained from the contemplation of this simple structure than from the most elaborate cathedral.

Elcho Island Church

ELCHO ISLAND (1900)

Glossary

ANGLE POSTS

BATTENS

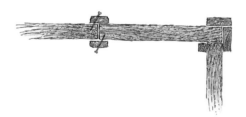

COB

ADOBE. A sun-dried brick, usually of sandy clay, or a wall made of such material.

ANGLE POSTS. Timber posts at the corners of a building.

ASHLAR STONEWORK. Walls built of carefully dressed and smoothed stones, laid in regular courses, with fine joints.

BARGEBOARD. A dressed board, sometimes ornamental, fixed on the face or edge of a gable, following the slope of the roof.

BATTENS. Narrow boards fixed over rafters for securing roof covering, or used to cover joints.

BEADED. Finished with a small, bead-like mould at the edge.

BOTTOM PLATE. The lowest horizontal piece of timber in a wall.

BRICK NOGGING. Brickwork laid between studs in a timber-framed wall or gable end. From Tudor half-timbered work.

BULL-NOSED IRON. Corrugated iron finished with a rounded end, used mainly over verandas.

BUTTRESS. A pier-like structure built against a wall to strengthen it, usually opposite a roof truss.

CAULKED. Made watertight by filling the joints with a soft material, as oakum is used in boat-building.

CHANCEL. The eastern end of an orthodox church, often separated from the body of the church by a railing.

CHIMNEY STALK. Generally that part of a chimney extending beyond the roof level.

CHISEL-DRAUGHTED MARGIN. A narrow edging on the face of a stone, smooth but still showing chisel marks.

CLAY PUG WALL. A wall made of clay mixed with water and worked into a mastic consistency.

COB. A mixture of clay and straw, packed and rammed, used either as blocks or between forming.

CONNECTORS. Various pieces of material, usually steel, used for joining two or more structural members.

CORRUGATED GALVANISED IRON. Iron or steel in sheet form, pressed to cause alternate ridges and troughs to increase its strength, then galvanised to resist rust.

COVED CEILING. A ceiling that does not connect directly with the top of the wall, but to rafters a short distance above the wall.

DOOR HEAD. The structural member (steel, timber, stone) that connects the two side pieces of a door frame and supports the wall above it.

EAVES. The overhang of a roof that serves to shade or otherwise protect the wall below it.

EMANCIPIST. A person who has been released from bondage or slavery or from legal restraints. In Australia, a released convict.

FASCIA. A plain flat band, such as that part of the eaves to which the gutter is attached.

PLATE

QUOINS

FLYING BUTTRESS. A buttress that is attached to a wall, usually at the top only and not for its full length.

FOOTINGS. The lowest part of a wall, usually wider than the thickness of the wall and sometimes wrongly called foundations.

GABLE. The upper triangular section of an end wall, with sides following the slope of the roof.

GATHERING. That portion of the chimney flue immediately above the fireplace which reduces the opening to the dimensions of the chimney stalk.

HAMMER BEAM. A short timber beam projecting from the top of a wall as partial support for a roof truss.

JOISTS. Framing timbers to which flooring or ceilings are fixed.

KING POST TRUSS. A roof truss in which there is one central vertical post, as distinct from a queen post truss (two) or a princess post truss (three).

LABEL MOULD. A projecting moulding over a door or window head to divert rainwater that may come down the face of the wall.

LANCET-ARCHED. An opening spanned by a pointed arch.

LAP AND SPACE CONSTRUCTION. A form in which wide boards or split slabs are used vertically, with narrow boards or battens over the joints.

MUD BRICKS. A term used to describe bricks made of a variety of materials such as clay, mud, coarse sand, etc., mixed with water and dried in the sun.

NOGGING. Short pieces of timber placed horizontally between wall studs.

PARAPET. That portion of a wall that projects above the roof line.

PLATE. The top and bottom members of a timber wall or almost any horizontal or sloping timber used to provide fixing for other timbers.

PISE. Various kinds of clay or mud mixed with water and rammed between forms.

PUG MORTAR. A mortar made from clay, mud, sand, cow manure, etc., used for laying bricks or stones.

QUOINS. Stones, usually dressed to exact dimensions, at the corners of a brick or stone building; or bricks, often projecting slightly beyond the wall face, to emphasise the corners or some other feature.

RAKING PARAPET. That portion of a wall projecting beyond the roof line and following the slope of the roof.

RAFTER. The main structural member in a roof.

REVEAL. The vertical side of an opening in a wall for a door or window.

ROCK-FACED STONE. The surface of a stone as it comes from a quarry.

SPLIT SLAB

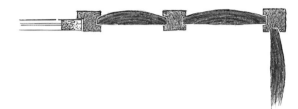

Part of a double-sided wattle and daub wall. This method of construction was used in the hut at Lexton, Victoria.

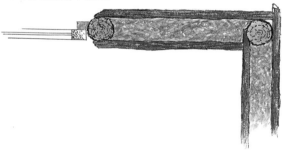

One method of log-cabin construction as was used in the miner's hut at Stuart Town, New South Wales.

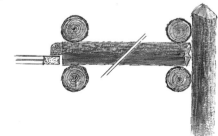

ROOF RIDGE. The topmost timber in a roof to which the rafters are secured.

ROOF TRUSS. A strong framework placed at intervals in a large roof as additional support.

SACRISTRY. That portion of a church building in which the sacred vessels are placed.

SAWN AND NOSED WEATHERBOARD. A sawn board that is not smoothly finished or dressed, with the lowest edge slightly rounded.

SHINGLES. Thin pieces of timber laid in overlapping rows to cover a roof. More correctly, a shake when used as split, a shingle when dressed after splitting.

SKILLION. A roof that slopes in one direction only.

SKIRTING. A piece of timber placed at the junction of wall and floor to cover any shrinkage.

SPARROW-PICKED STONE. The face of a stone first smoothed and then pitted at close intervals as though pecked by a bird.

SPLAYED. Finished at an angle as distinct from having a squared end, or wider at one end than the other.

SPLIT SLAB. A slab split from a log so that it is roughly smooth on one face and slightly rounded on the other.

STUDS. The vertical members in a timber-framed wall or gable end.

TENONED. Trimmed at the end to fit into a mortise or square hole.

TICKET-OF-LEAVE MAN. A convict who, on account of good behaviour, is on probationary release.

TONGUE AND GROOVED. A board with a projection of one-third its thickness on one edge (tongue) and grooved on the other edge to receive the tongue on the adjoining board.

TOOLED MARGIN. A finish to a stone very similar to a chisel-draughted margin.

TOP PLATE. The horizontal member on top of a wall.

TRENCH. A continuous recess cut in a bottom plate to receive split slabs or other wall members.

VERANDA PLATE. The beam connecting the tops of veranda posts and carrying the rafters or roof structure.

VERMICULATED. A form of stone finish having thin raised portions simulating worm tracks.

WAINSCOT. Panelling or lining to the lower part of a wall, primarily intended to prevent damage by chair backs.

WEATHERBOARDS. External cladding made up of a number of overlapping boards placed horizontally.

WHITTLED PEGS. Wooden pegs with points shaped by a knife, used to hold saplings together.

WINDOW REVEALS. The vertical sides of a window opening in a wall.